ADVENTUROUS PUB WALKS
IN
NORFOLK

Will Martin

COUNTRYSIDE BOOKS
NEWBURY BERKSHIRE

COUNTRYSIDE BOOKS
3 Catherine Road
Newbury, Berkshire

To view our complete range of books,
please visit us at
www.countrysidebooks.co.uk

ISBN 1 85306 782 2

Designed by Peter Davies, Nautilus Design
Maps originated by Lynne Martin
Photographs by the author

Produced through MRM Associates Ltd., Reading
Printed by J. W. Arrowsmith Limited, Bristol

CONTENTS

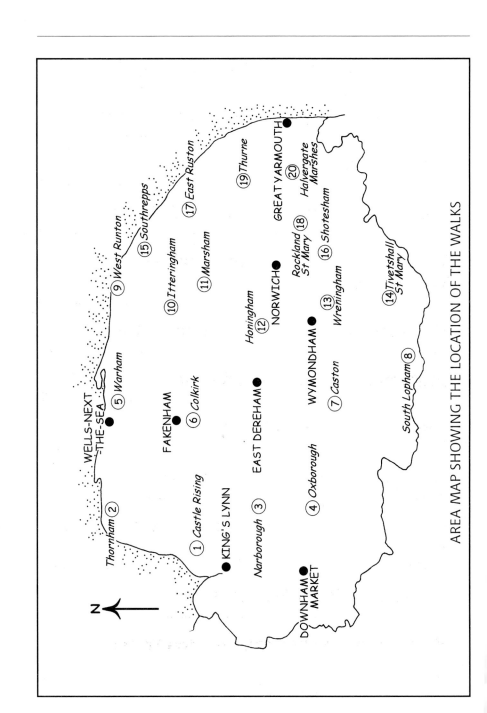

AREA MAP SHOWING THE LOCATION OF THE WALKS

N

Thornham ②

① Castle Rising
KING'S LYNN ●

Narborough ③

④ Oxborough

DOWNHAM
MARKET ●

WELLS-NEXT
-THE-SEA ●

⑤ Warham

FAKENHAM ●
⑥ Colkirk

EAST DEREHAM ●

⑨ West Runton

⑮ Southrepps

⑩ Itteringham

⑪ Marsham

Honingham
⑫
NORWICH ●

WYMONDHAM ●

⑦ Caston

South Lopham
⑧

⑰ East Ruston

⑲ Thurne

GREAT YARMOUTH ●

Rockland ⑱
St Mary

⑯ Shotesham

Halvergate
Marshes
⑳

⑬
Wreningham

⑭ Tivetshall/
St Mary

INTRODUCTION

'Adventure' is perhaps not the first word that springs to mind in connection with sleepy old Norfolk . . . but it all depends on how you look at it.

It's true that I can't offer you the muscle-straining, calf-killing slogs you could find in other parts of the country – Noel Coward's often quoted, and derided, words 'very flat, Norfolk' still have more than a touch of truth about them. But these circular walks based on good pubs, serving good food, are certainly long enough and demanding enough to present a challenge, though you don't have to be super-fit to tackle them.

There are also adventures and enjoyments of a different kind to be had, chief among which is a journey into the past, into a landscape that often seems unchanged and unchanging. Here, quiet villages with their traditional flint cottages and modestly beautiful churches are reached on narrow lanes still relatively free of traffic, or on grassy footways with a distant origin. Here, there are ancient grazing marshes and water meadows, slow-moving rivers with mirror reflections of vast skies, stretches of sandy heathland backed by walls of dark-green conifer.

There is an adventure, too, into a world of wildlife, especially birds, that is unrivalled in England. Several of these long walks will take you close to saltmarsh and estuary that are favoured places of the waders, and where flocks can be seen twisting and turning as one creature, silver underwings flashing as they catch the light.

As for the many excellent, historic pubs of Norfolk, I cannot claim these are exactly an adventure – though along with the warm welcome which I believe you will find, there is the chance to sample a fine range of locally brewed, and perhaps unfamiliar, beers as well as food which often uses fresh ingredients from the surrounding sea and countryside. All the landlords and landladies of the featured pubs are happy to let customers use their car parks while they are walking but would expect notification, either by phone or in person, so that they know how many vehicles and people are involved. Many of these pubs are open all day and you will be able to reward yourself with a meal whenever (within reason) you return from your walk. Telephone numbers are given so that you can check the opening times at all the establishments and plan your day accordingly. Because the Berney Arms in Walk 20 has no access by road, this route starts elsewhere and reaches the pub en route. If you prefer to stop for a meal rather than a picnic during your walks it will be easy for you to settle on an alternative, though park carefully if you leave your car by the roadside and make sure that you are not blocking exits or entrances.

Most of the walks cross farmland at some point and so the usual countryside courtesies are important, such as closing gates behind you. Footpath signs are not, regettably, as evident as they should be, though I have reported all the cases that would benefit from one, or where one has obviously been broken and lost. The situation is constantly being updated and there may be improvements made after the time of writing.

Because on several of these walks there is little in the way of shade or shelter, it is especially important to have the right clothing – good walking boots are essential, as is a set of waterproofs, in which I would include overtrousers, and a hat as protection from the sun. Layers of thinner garments are better than one thick one, as they allow you to change according to the weather as you go along. A bottle of water is also a must.

Good walking!

Will Martin

PUBLISHER'S NOTE

We hope that you obtain considerable enjoyment from this book; great care has been taken in its preparation. However, changes of landlord and actual closures of pubs are sadly not uncommon. Likewise, although at the time of publication all routes followed public rights of way or permitted paths, diversion orders can be made and permissions withdrawn.

We cannot, of course, be held responsible for such diversion orders and any inaccuracies in the text which result from these or any other changes to the routes nor any damage which might result from walkers trespassing on private property. We are anxious though that all details covering the walks and the pubs are kept up to date and would therefore welcome information from readers that would be relevant to future editions.

The sketch maps accompanying each walk are not always to scale and are intended to guide you to the starting point and give a simple but accurate idea of the route to be taken. For those who like the benefit of detailed maps, we recommend that you arm yourself with the relevant Ordnance Survey map in either the Landranger, Outdoor Leisure or Explorer series.

CASTLE RISING, CONGHAM AND ROYDON COMMON NATURE RESERVE

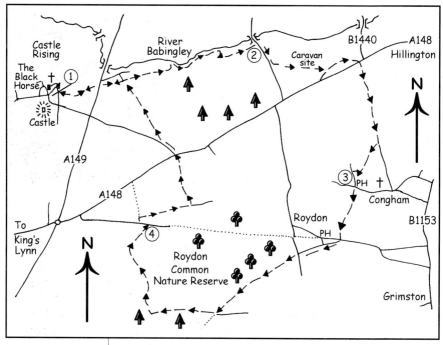

Distance:
9½ miles

Map: OS Landranger 132 or Explorer 250

Starting Point:
The Black Horse Inn. GR 666248

How to get there: *Castle Rising is 3 miles north-east of King's Lynn, signed left off the A149 going towards Hunstanton. The Black Horse Inn is in the village centre, near the church.*

THE 'FLYING FLOCK' OF SHEEP ON ROYDON COMMON

'Rising was a sea-port town, where Lynn was but a marsh. Now Lynn is a sea-port town, and Rising fares the worse.' The old saying may indicate a decline in the fortunes of Castle Rising village – as well as its modern distance from the sea – but it still makes a fine place to start a walk. You have to grit your teeth as you cross two main roads streaming with holiday traffic in summer, but the contrast with lovely, unspoilt countryside then seems all the sharper. Most of the walk is through an uncultivated landscape, rare enough in Norfolk, and takes in a large stretch of Roydon Common – one of the county's outstanding wildlife habitats.

The Black Horse Inn is a handsome, red-brick building which has had a varied life; from its early days when a tenant named Moyes was replaced in 1809 as 'his affairs got so embarrassed he could not continue' up to recent years when it has changed from regular pub to restaurant chain family diner and back again.

The dining pub legacy is a huge restaurant area – 120 seats – but divided up by brick pillars and archways into beamed and attractively decorated sections. And there is still plenty of room for drinkers in the comfortable main bar, with its chintzy chairs and sofas, and an adjoining wooden-floored room with a dartboard and village local atmosphere.

Food is traditional pub grub, virtually all home-cooked – steak and kidney pudding, a range of Black Horse hotpots such as steak and walnut, cottage pie, harvest veg and leek crumble – plus popular foreign dishes including Cajun chicken and lasagne 'de la Castile'. There is a good range of 'hob rolls' and sandwiches, with fillings that include crab from Cromer or Wells.

Real ales on offer are Adnams Broadside, Woodforde's Wherry, Shepherd Neame Spitfire and Morland Old Speckled Hen plus guests such as Wychwood Reaper. Outside there is a large patio/garden area in a pleasant spot opposite the church, and the pub is open all day in summer, with long food hours.
Telephone: 01553 631225.

The Walk

Castle Rising's glory days were centred mainly on the castle itself with its magnificent keep built in 1138 and home to aristocracy and royalty – notably Queen Isabella, wife of Edward II. The building is still in good shape near the centre of this attractive village built of local carrstone, which also has St Lawrence's church with a fine Norman west porch and the almshouses of Trinity Hospital, built in 1614 for 20 spinsters 'of good character'. The women living there still wear distinctive costumes with black, pointed hats on ceremonial occasions.

① Coming out of the car park at the rear of the pub, turn left and follow the road as it bends round to the right. Immediately after a pair of pretty carrstone cottages on the left, one of them called Rising Winds, turn left with a fingerpost on a footpath between houses. This leads out into open country and climbs gradually with attractive meadowland to the right and then bends left, with the **Sandringham Estate's** tall, Italianate water tower ahead in the distance, to the A149. Cross this busy coast road, turn left for a few yards and take a path heading into woodland, following a fingerpost. The narrow path bends slightly right down a bank to cross a ditch on a plank bridge and then veers slightly left to head between silver birches and conifers. There was a large tree down across the path when I was here, but it was easy enough to go round it and continue. Cross a second plank bridge and at a T-junction of paths turn left then, after a few yards, right onto a gravel track. Pass Mill House Cottage on the left and where the track bends sharp left, keep ahead on a broad,

unsigned path into trees. This is now a lovely, shady path through mixed woodland that is managed as a conservation area where native red squirrels have been reintroduced. The path is now at variance with the OS map as you come out of the wood; go over a stile and stay ahead along the right-hand side of the meadow, with trees on your right. There is a more obvious path heading diagonally left across the meadow but I found this led to a gate that was tied shut. At the end of the field, go over a combination stile, bridge with handrail and second stile, then turn immediately left on a path that is not clearly defined but stays close to a

THE BLACK HORSE INN

barbed-wire fence. At the riverbank, turn right on a grassy track, again not clearly defined at first but staying close to the water for a good distance. This is the **Babingley**, a slow-flowing river as pretty as its name which leads through rough meadowland popular with birds of prey – we saw a barn owl, a couple of kestrels and a fleeting glimpse of what I thought was a hobby on our walk. Go over a stile and shortly the path turns right, away from the river, through a metal gate and left along a broad track with a cropfield to the right to meet a lane. (2¼ miles)

② Turn right along the lane and after about 400 yards left on a broad, unsigned track with a hedge on the left and heading past a caravan site. I saw a mixed flock of greenfinches, goldfinches and chaffinches feeding on linseed pods in the field to the right, their wings flashing colour. Stay ahead as the track becomes gravelled then turn left on a lane that curves round to meet the A148. Cross and turn left for a few yards before turning right past a carrstone house onto a metalled track signed 'private driveway and public bridleway'. This twists and turns past the brick piers of an old railway line then, as the driveway bends left towards a house, the now unsurfaced track veers right with a public bridleway fingerpost through woodland. Keep ahead with a Norfolk County Council blue arrow, ignoring a path to the right, then

shortly after the end of the wood turn right with a yellow arrow on a path along a field edge which bends left and right across a plank bridge. Go over a second bridge then turn sharp left with a yellow arrow on a broad, grassy path along a field edge. This runs into a concrete track past farm buildings and cottages on the right to meet a lane. Just to the left here is the **Anvil** pub, whose front garden looking onto a peaceful lane makes a good refreshment stop. (2 miles)

③ Turn right at the junction and after 20 yards, opposite a house called The Birches, turn left with a fingerpost on a clear path cut through a cropfield. Head into the next field with a yellow arrow and the path bends right and left over a plank bridge into woodland. Go over a stile and across a meadow heading for a modern, red-roofed house. Climb another stile alongside the house to meet a road, with the **Three Horseshoes** pub just a few yards to the right. Cross the road and a green then turn right onto a lane, ignoring a footpath straight ahead. Pass a mixture of old and new houses, then, at a junction, cross **Chapel Road** and keep ahead through a wooden gate onto a grassy path with a dyke on the left and woodland to your right.

You are now on Roydon Common, managed by Norfolk Wildlife Trust and one of the most interesting habitats in the county, with unusual plants, including orchids and sundews, and many birds including breeding curlews. There are also free-ranging horses which you may well pass along the way, as we did, and you could see the NWT's 'Flying Flock' of grazing Shetland and Black Welsh Mountain sheep, which is moved around various reserves in Norfolk to keep the vegetation down for wildlife.

The attractive, shady path broadens before leading to a wooden kissing gate which you go through and turn right on a track past the **Railway Gatehouse** with damp woodland on both sides. The sandy track leads uphill, passing a path to the left, then in a few more yards you turn right through a spring-loaded metal gate where there is an older **Roydon Common Nature Reserve** board. This is now a delightful path with a fine view over undulating heathland purple with heather in summer, an unusual landscape for Norfolk. The path bends left to a junction with a broad, sandy track. Turn right here, over a cattle grid to meet a road. (3 miles)

④ Turn left on the road and after 100 yards right onto a path with a partially hidden fingerpost along a field edge. After 50 yards turn right with a yellow arrow on a grassy path with cropfields rising to the skyline on your left and a hedge on the right. Keep ahead where the path runs into a broader track, which then veers right and ahead up a field with the hedge now on the left. Where this meets the elbow of a much broader track, turn left with a yellow arrow and head up a gradual slope between banks of bracken. This pleasant track leads into a concreted hard-standing by the A148, which you cross onto a shady lane that soon leads downhill. Where the lane bends left, turn right with a fingerpost onto a path heading into woodland where there is a board detailing the red squirrel project. Eventually turn left with a fingerpost onto the path that you covered early in the walk. Go through the wood and recross the A149, retracing your steps through the fields and turning right at the lane to return to the pub. (2¼ miles)

Date walk completed:

THORNHAM, THE PEDDARS WAY AND GORE POINT

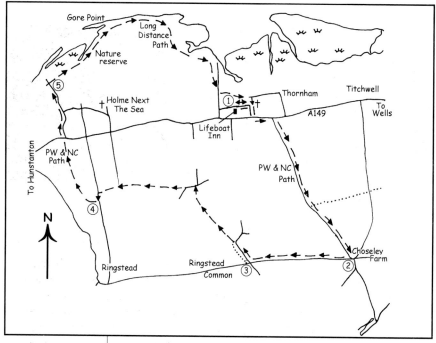

Distance:
10 miles

Map: OS Landranger 132 or Explorer 250

Starting Point:
The Lifeboat Inn.
GR 729435

How to get there: *Thornham is 4 miles east of Hunstanton on the A149 coast road. From that direction the Lifeboat Inn is on a back road near the entrance to the village and is signed left off the main road.*

THORNHAM HARBOUR

I know people who feel uneasy out in the openness of the Norfolk saltmarshes, who find the twisting creeks and channels cut into the featureless landscape slightly scary. For all of them – as well as for the rest of us who love the silver-streaked marshland – this walk offers the ideal compromise as you get to see it from above without becoming too closely involved. First comes a splendid track along a ridge with the coast spread out before you, then an unusual boardwalk through the sand dunes with the sea below, and finally a long bank which, again, gives you a fine view across the surrounding marsh.

The Lifeboat Inn is a substantial white-painted pub. You may feel slightly apprehensive as you approach, having read its own description, '16th century smugglers' ale house', but, once inside, it is clear the place does have a genuine and most appealing period atmosphere.

The cosy Smugglers Bar, with its chalk-lump walls, scrubbed wooden tables and antique paraffin lamps hung among an assortment of guns and marshman's tools, was indeed used by smugglers to divide up their spoils. Leading off it are two tiny 'Duck or Grouse' snugs and beyond those a galleried central lobby with imposing fireplace and a large traditionally-styled restaurant. There are two conservatories, one hung with a vine; two patios, one of them paved and particularly well planted to provide shade; and a screened children's play area.

The standard menu and specials board together offer a wide choice of food, much of it using fresh local produce, with fish especially well represented. Dishes could include garlic and coriander crevettes; Lifeboat fish pie with prawns, smoked haddock, salmon and cod; baked fillet of sea bass; panfried lamb cutlets with olive mash. Veggies are well catered for, with such dishes as spicy five-bean chilli; and spinach and mozarella lasagne, and there are also five ploughman's plus a good range of filled baguettes.

Real ales in this freehouse number at least five, the regulars being Adnams, Greene King IPA and Abbot and Woodforde's Wherry plus a guest. Thirteen wines are sold by the glass.
Overnight accommodation is available in 14 ensuite rooms, most with superb views across the saltmarsh.
Telephone 01485 512236.

The Walk

Thornham, like many places along the North Norfolk coast, once had an active sea trade in coal and corn from a harbour that is now just a narrow creek. It was a popular place with smugglers, who used to sink their contraband in waterproof containers and then recover the goods when the tide had receded. Nowadays artists and birdwatchers are drawn to the beauty of the village setting.

① Turn left out of the car park and along the lane, passing in front of the pub. The view left across the saltmarsh to the sea is a taste of things to come. At the T-junction, turn right to the main road, where you turn left past **All Saints' church** onto the High Street. A constant stream of holiday traffic in summer must make life difficult for the residents of this attractive village, with its many traditional flint cottages. Pass the village sign showing Thornham's boating and metalworking heritage then take the next lane on the right, **Choseley Road**. You soon leave the houses behind as the lane, little used by traffic and part of the long-distance **Norfolk Coast Path**, climbs steadily towards the skyline. To the left there is a fine view back down towards the lagoons of the RSPB's **Titchwell bird reserve** and the sea beyond. As you reach the brow of the hill, rolling farmland stretches away on both sides where there are good

numbers of hares – as we sat for a rest by a field edge just off the road during a summertime walk, one of these splendid animals approached to within a few feet of us before disappearing into the crop of wheat. The lane now dips and climbs again towards **Choseley Farm** where, at a junction immediately after a row of three brick-built cottages, you turn right. (2¼ miles)

② The road now stretches long and straight ahead of you but, sadly, cannot be avoided as there is no footpath anywhere near. The consolations are that, again, this is about as far removed from the coast

THE 16TH CENTURY PUB IN THORNHAM

road in terms of traffic as you can get, there is a walkable grass verge for part of the way with views to the right over undulating farmland and, above all, there is the thought of the reward you will shortly reap for all this footslogging. I have often thought that if I were a farmer I would put in permissive footpaths by long stretches of road where there is no alternative route – in this case, one along the field edge just the other side of the hedge would make so much difference. Eventually, at a crossroads, turn right over a stile onto a path that runs to the left of the lane, with a **Peddars Way** Circular Walks arrow. (1¼ miles)

③ The grassy path leads alongside a stunningly beautiful wildflower meadow – this has clearly been planted and I am hopeful it will look like this for many years to come with its summertime spread of cornflower, poppy, scabious, marjoram, corn marigold, clover and vetch among others. On a sunny day scores of butterflies, especially common blues, were enjoying it as much as we were. Go through a wooden gate at the end of the meadow and turn left onto a broad, grassy track, still with the Circular Walks arrow. This is a lovely path that climbs steadily with open fields to the right until at the top of the slope, where the track meets a junction of lanes, it seems that the whole of the North Norfolk coast is spread out below you. On a clear day

such as we had, you can easily see Lincolnshire over the Wash to your left, with the villages of **Thornham** and **Holme next the Sea** in front of you. Turn left on the lane and after 150 yards, where it bends left, stay ahead on the grassy track. This is a fine stretch of pathway believed to date back to Iron Age times, along a ridge with outstanding views to the coast and a wonderful feeling of freedom. I was lucky enough last time to see a buzzard here – not a common bird in Norfolk – circling on a thermal high above. Eventually the track meets a lane where you turn left and then after 150 yards, just past the **Ringstead** village name sign and with the mill ahead, right with a Peddars Way fingerpost and acorn marker. (2 miles)

④ The well-trodden path runs along a field edge and bends sharply right, soon passing an engraved stone slab.

This is one of five newish markers alongside the Peddars Way, carved by Tom Perkins and quoting from a text by Hugh Lupton. The aim, detailed in the book 'A Norfolk Songline' (Hickathrift Books 2000) is 'to bring to the surface the layers that are held in the memory of the sand, soil, flint, peat, chalk, clay and carrstone beneath our feet'.

The path now heads downhill, becoming broader and shadier between hedges, to meet the main road where you cross and stay ahead on the lane with a Peddars fingerpost pointing you towards **Holme Beach**. Keep straight on, ignoring the lane to the right leading into Holme next the Sea (where there is the White Horse pub), and along the narrow village green, then over the golf course with its warning about flying balls. (1¾ miles)

⑤ The sea is now only just ahead of you over the dunes if you fancy a detour at this stage – though there will be other opportunities to wiggle your toes in the sand – as you turn right onto a path with the acorn sign. Lavender Marsh is now between you and the sea, pale purple with sea-lavender in summer and etched by channels of water. Just before the path bends left towards the sea, head up the bank on your right to an arched brick Norfolk Naturalists Trust donation box and a warning sign about the dangerous tides along this stretch of coast around **Gore Point**. Turn left with an acorn marker along a boardwalk that continues now for a good distance over the dunes. This is another fine path with the sea to your left – this area of beach is where the mysterious 4,000 year old

wooden circle known as **Seahenge** was discovered (now removed for conservation) – and the saltmarshes of **Holme Dunes Nature Reserve** stretching away to your right. The path comes very close to the beach and then passes the nature reserve centre to the right – open daily from 10 am to 5 pm and selling refreshments – before heading through a small conifer plantation. Emerging from the trees, turn right up wooden steps to the **Holme Bird Observatory** and left along the boardwalk with lagoons to your right below. The path bends right inland past **Ragged Marsh**, left along a bank and right again. Stay ahead, with the boats of Thornham harbour and car park over to your left, and the path soon leads down a slope to join a lane. Turn right and after a few yards left, with the Peddars marker, on a path that twists over the saltmarsh to meet the elbow of a lane, where you turn right and right again back to the pub. If the sight of the Lifeboat Inn ahead of you is too tempting by this stage, miss out this last stretch of footpath and simply go straight down the lane and left to the pub. (2¾ miles)

Date walk completed:

_____

NARBOROUGH, MARHAM FEN AND THE NAR VALLEY WAY

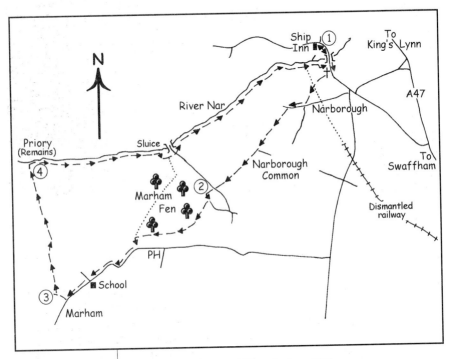

Distance:

8¼ miles

Starting Point:

The Ship Inn car park. GR 746134

MAP: OS Landranger 132 or Explorer 236

How to get there: *Narborough is 10 miles south-east of King's Lynn, signed just off the A47. Coming from Lynn, turn right into the village and the pub stands on the right, at a junction with the road to Pentney.*

SWANS ON THE TRANQUIL RIVER NAR

*T*here are many riverside walks in Norfolk but, unless you are a boat fanatic, this is one of the best. The River Nar shows little sign of its busy past and is a delight to look at as you walk along, with its crystal-clear water and lush vegetation. Before that, you start the walk in the ancient village of Narborough – in the Domesday Book as Nereburh, probably meaning 'fortified place at a narrow pass' – which does still have signs of an industrial heritage in its maltings and mill. The walk also takes in farmland, whose light soil is ideal for root crops such as carrots and parsnips, and a lovely stretch of grassy track alongside woodland at Marham Fen.

The Ship Inn was built in the 1740s. It is a reminder of Narborough's thriving past, especially its transport links – the turnpike road from King's Lynn ended there, the railway ran close by and barges unloaded at the staithe only yards away. This handsome cream and black painted pub may have lost its old-style river trade but it can at least count many fishermen among its customers, as the popular Narborough Trout Lakes are just across the road and the catch, naturally, is featured on the menu.

The pub's cosy main bar has a distinctly ship-like feel to it, with its wood-panelled walls, low beamed ceiling and large model of Drake's *Golden Hind* above the painted brick fireplace. A brass plaque with the words 'Captain's Cabin' on the bar finishes off the illusion nicely. There is also a games room, with pool table and dartboard, and off the entrance lobby an attractive dining room which also serves as a breakfast room for guests in the six double bedrooms.

The food is largely traditional English pub grub, the house speciality being a varying range of homemade plate pies – steak and Guinness or chicken, leek and Stilton, for example. There is usually a daily special such as lamb shank, vegetarian dishes are available, and the range of 'doorstep' sandwiches is especially popular.

> **Real ales** *in this freehouse are Greene King IPA, John Smith's Cask Bitter and a guest such as Morland Old Speckled Hen or Marston's Pedigree.*
> *Outside there is a small beer garden by the river and a gravelled patio area.*
> *Telephone: 01760 337307.*

 *The Walk*

Across the road from the pub, and worth a look before you start, is the Narborough village sign, in the shape of a wheel that survived from the old bone mill where bones were crushed for fertiliser; the spokes divide it into segments, each depicting an aspect of village life. One of these is Narborough Hall, former home of the Spelman family perhaps best remembered now for Sir John Spelman, a lawyer who took part in the trial of Sir Thomas More and prepared the indictment that brought Anne Boleyn to the block in 1536. Also shown are the parish church; the corn mill; the maltings; a train crossing a bridge – the line closed in 1968; and a First World War plane flying over a hangar – Narborough then had one of the largest aerodromes in Britain, home to hundreds of officers and men of the Royal Flying Corps.

① Turn right out of the pub car park and, at the junction, right on the road towards the village centre. Pass the old maltings on the right then cross the **River Nar** with the former mill across the road to your left. Immediately before **All Saints' church** with its fine east window, turn right onto a fingerposted path that runs alongside the churchyard and then past gardens. The path soon bends left to head through a cropfield, over the line of the long-dismantled railway and, after a further 150 yards, meets the bend of the lane. Turn right here onto a track with a blue bridleway arrow and fingerpost, soon passing a copse of poplars on the left. Where the track bends right onto private land, take a broad footpath heading diagonally left, still with the bridleway arrow, across a cropfield towards a belt of conifers. A swathe of set-aside land here was covered, as we passed, in summer, with the striking blue flowers of what I think was a variety of valerian. Go through the tree-belt and keep ahead, soon ignoring a path to the left. Where the main track bends right, stay ahead on a grassier path with a hedge on your left. Dark-brown ringlet butterflies danced along the path ahead of us here. Cross a wooden footbridge over a ditch and keep ahead between

THE HANDSOME SHIP INN AT NARBOROUGH

cropfields, with a double row of saplings on your left, to meet a track. (2 miles)

② Turn left here and, after 50 yards, right onto a broad path following a white bridle route arrow. Woodland is now on the right and open fields to the left, with the buildings of the extensive **RAF Marham** airbase in the distance beyond.

Unless you are a plane buff, weekends are the best times to do this walk when there is normally no flying, as Marham has expanded to become the RAF's largest operational base in the UK, home to five squadrons, including four of Tornados, and 6,000 people.

Cross a track and go through a metal gate with a public footpath fingerpost onto a delightful path that skirts the damp woodland of **Marham Fen**. The woodland edge here is rich in birdlife, with groups of blue, great and long-tailed tits active and noisy in the treetops. The path takes a gradual curve to the right, eventually leading through a metal gate onto a track where you turn left, past a few modern houses to a T-junction with a road, where you turn right. A short distance up the road to the left at this point is the Fox and Hounds pub, should you need refreshment. Stay on the road towards **Marham** village as it bends first right then left.

Here we were lucky enough to see a barn owl, carrying a mouse in its claws, fly through a hole in the roof of an old chapel. It no doubt had a nest there, but since the building had a 'Sold' sign outside – for conversion to a house, I expect – it would have to be looking for somewhere else in the near future.

Pass the school, set back from the road on the left, then the cemetery and 100 yards or so beyond that, turn right onto Fen Lane. (2 miles)

③ As the lane ends, turn right through a metal gate then head diagonally right following the direction of a public footpath fingerpost. After 50 yards you enter a long stretch of meadowland where another footpath sign would be very handy. However, head diagonally right and up the grassy ride with a hedge on your left and denser woodland to the right. Keep close to the hedge, following the line of a dyke that soon becomes visible on your left. At the end of the field, go through a metal gate on the left and keep ahead on the path leading straight towards the River Nar, first between hedges then with open fields on the left and the dyke now on the right – not the left, as it appears on the map. This section may not be easy as the path can be badly overgrown, depending on the time of year, but a useful marker to aim for is the castellated tower of the

Pentney priory ruin, which is on the other side of the river and soon becomes visible straight ahead of you. Your reward comes eventually when you head up the bank and turn right over a stile onto the broad path by the River Nar. This is perhaps Norfolk's least-known major river and one of its prettiest, with its clear water flowing lazily over a chalk bed and reed-fringed banks on either side. (1¼ miles)

④ You are now on the **Nar Valley Way**, a long-distance footpath from King's Lynn to Gressenhall, near Dereham, and the path follows the river all the way back to Narborough.

It is hard to imagine now, looking at the narrow, tranquil river, that in the 19th century it was busy with barge traffic carrying coal and timber up from King's Lynn and malt and corn back down. Soon you reach a stretch where the river was straightened to make this trade easier. No boats use it now and it has become a wildlife corridor, rich in flowers, birds and butterflies. Almost as soon as we joined the river path last time, an oystercatcher flew overhead with its insistent, piping call; at the top of one nearby bush, only inches apart, a male yellowhammer and a yellow wagtail vied with each other to be the brighter bird and a barn owl – perhaps the one we had seen earlier – drifted over the fields away towards Marham.

The path leads past a sluice where you have to divert right and left round the pumping station, then back beside the river, soon passing an old waterwheel on the opposite bank. This is now a particularly lovely stretch of the walk, with an abundance of wildflowers in season, summertime butterflies everywhere and, soon, swans on the water too. Eventually the path bends right to follow a channel off the river then turns right behind houses. At the cul-de-sac road, turn right and left back to the main road, where you turn left back to the pub. (3 miles)

Date walk completed:

OXBOROUGH, GOODERSTONE AND BEACHAMWELL

THE SEMI-RUINED CHURCH OF ST JOHN THE EVANGELIST, OXBOROUGH

Distance:
10¼ miles

Map: OS Landranger 143 or Explorer 236

Starting Point:
The Bedingfield Coach House inn. GR 745015

How to get there: *Oxborough is 7 miles west of Downham Market, just off the A134. The Bedingfield Coach House inn stands by a crossroads in the village centre.*

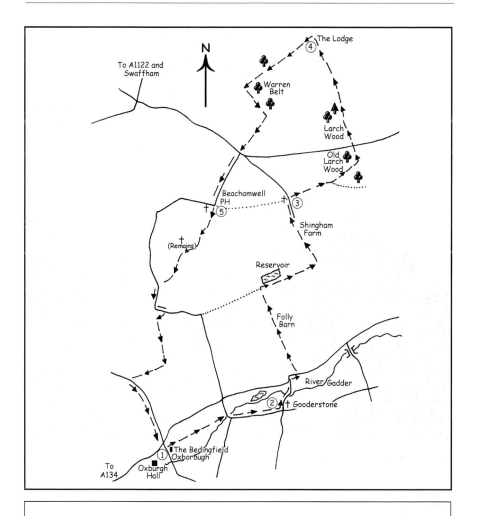

_T_he Breckland area of West Norfolk has a character and a quiet charm all its own. For centuries sandy semi-desert where only rabbits thrived, the 'broken land' of the name was tamed in the 18th century by the widespread planting of pines as windbreaks to allow cultivation. How successful a policy it was can be seen on this exhilarating walk on good, straight tracks under enormous skies. There is a sense of timeless tranquillity here, with little traffic on the lanes and an abundance of wildlife to cheer you as you pass.

The Bedingfield Coach House is in a lovely spot overlooking the green. This inn is around 200 years old and formerly belonged to the Bedingfields of nearby Oxburgh Hall. By 1845 it was known as the Spread Eagle – the family crest features this bird – and at some stage during the last century it became the Bedingfield Arms. After closure and extensive renovation it hatched out in 2002 as the Coach House, which probably reflects an earlier use. An attractive period feel has been achieved in the main bar with its wooden floor, brick fireplace, black beams and terracotta walls, and also in the two smaller dining rooms – one non-smoking – off to the sides.

The food, cooked to order, is described as English-based with a European influence, the keynote being a high quality of produce, much of it local. Traditional dishes such as bangers with Cheddar mash, and steak and mushroom pie rub shoulders with lemon and coriander duck breast, and the Coach House curry ('not for the faint-hearted'). Vegetarian options could include spinach and potato pie with roasted vegetables, and there is also a range of baguettes. Food is not served on Monday evenings.

Real ales in this freehouse are Greene King IPA, Fuller's London Pride and Morland Old Speckled Hen.
There is a pleasant beer garden at the side of the pub. Overnight accommodation is available in three ensuite bedrooms.
Telephone: 01366 328300.

The Walk

① Turn right out of the pub car park and down the lane, passing **Chantry House** on the right and the old post office on the left. After a further 20 yards turn right on a path between houses, following a public footpath fingerpost. Go over a stile and turn left along the field edge. After 100 yards cross a track and keep ahead on a grassy path with a hedge on your right. A rippling barley field just beginning to acquire its reddish tinge was a delight as I passed. After 400 yards go over a stile to the right and keep along the left-hand edge of the meadow, taking care not to trip over the rabbits that seem to be everywhere. As you approach the end of the field, head diagonally for the right-hand corner and go over a stile onto the lane. Turn right and follow the lane as it bends left, over the **River Gadder** and into the village of **Gooderstone**, with its mixture of modern bungalows and attractive flint cottages. (1 ¼ miles)

② Turn left immediately before St George's church onto Clarke's Lane, a quiet, shady road with a dyke on the right edged with wildflowers.

The church, with its squat flint tower and unusual diamond-shaped clock face is mainly 14th century, though the oldest part is said to go back 1,000 years. Inside, it is light and airy, and noticeable features include an ancient alms box and the mechanism of the old church clock on display.

At the T-junction, turn right on the road and, after 100 yards, left onto a broad track with a (somewhat overgrown) fingerpost. A footpath that now looks tempting on the map, heading diagonally right across fields of potatoes – a major crop in this part of Breckland – has obviously been ploughed up, so keep ahead on the pleasant, grassy track with the hedge on your left. You may well see hares now – I noticed four together, and before that one dashed out almost from under my feet – and over to the right is a line of the gnarled pines, black against the skyline, that are so typical of the area. Pass Folly Barn on the right and then, at a T-junction, turn right onto a sandy track, passing the banks of an irrigation reservoir on your left. You

THE PUB IN OXBOROUGH

may not be able to see the water but in summer you can enjoy the stunning aerobatics of house martins taking advantage of its insect population. After passing through a belt of trees, ignore a yellow arrow marker to the left and keep ahead between open fields to another T-junction. Turn left on the track, soon passing **Shingham Farm** on the right with its chequerwork flint frontage as the track becomes a lane. (2½ miles)

There is now on the left a small, unnamed church set back from the lane which has a beautiful carved stone door arch and a simple, grassed churchyard that makes a pleasant place for a rest stop.

③ Just after passing the church, turn right with a fingerpost and a yellow marker past a row of cottages. (To cut the walk to 6 miles, turn diagonally left just past the church onto a path, with a fingerpost, through a meadow to **Beachamwell** where you rejoin the main walk just past the Great Dane's Head pub.) Keep ahead with a hedge on your right and a large pig farm on the left. Where the track bends left and right, veer right and head along the edge of a cropfield, now with the hedge on your left. Smile ruefully (or scowl as the mood takes you) as you pass a yellow arrow pointing diagonally and optimistically right with no sign of a path and keep ahead, between two posts and along a path with

woodland on either side. After 300 yards this emerges onto a lane where you turn left, passing the **Old Larch Wood** with its fine array of conifers of many different species. Away to the right now is typical Breckland scenery, its windbreak belts of dark-green conifers contrasting with the lighter greens of the extensive cropfields. At the T-junction of lanes, cross and keep ahead, now with a blue bridleway arrow and fingerpost, onto a pleasant track with woodland on the left and open fields to the right. After 300 yards where the track forks, keep right to pass a handsome flint house on the left, then stay ahead, ignoring a path off to the right. At the wood's end, go through a metal gate and onto a track where partridges will quite likely trot ahead as the wonderful feeling of openness under the huge skies makes you feel like striding out in pursuit. The path soon runs alongside woodland on the right, then bends left and right past ruined buildings to meet a broader track. (2 miles)

④ Now turn left, passing a house with diamond-paned windows on the right. After half a mile, the track passes a belt of trees called Nursery Plantation on the right, then the woodland of **Warren Belt** on the left. Immediately after this, turn left on an unsigned but clear path running alongside the trees. The need for these windbreaks is now obvious as you see the sandy nature of the soil, which would otherwise be whisked away in the stiff breeze that often blows here. At the end of the wood, follow the main track round to the right between fields with their giant hose reels for crop irrigation. Pass farm buildings on the left and at a junction of lanes keep ahead, signed to Beachamwell, on **Chestnut Walk**, which is indeed lined by sweet chestnuts as well as a good grass verge for walking. Pass modern housing developments on both sides and then stay ahead on Old Hall Lane with the **Great Dane's Head** pub on the left. This looks like a place with a split personality – the sign over the front door shows a large dog's head while the hanging sign by the road has the head of a rather fearsome (and doubtless historically more appropriate) Danish warrior on one side but, intriguingly, the name Hole in the Wall on the other. (1¾ miles)

⑤ The lane soon turns into a track with a fingerpost and leads through a metal gate with the large Hall Barn conversion on the right. Cross a meadow with the almost-vanished remains of **All Saints' church** on the right and go through a metal gate as the path bends right. Immediately head diagonally left for 20 yards across the corner of a field, or skirt it if the crop is too tall, to pick up a clear grassy track leading across the rough meadow. The path bends right with a yellow arrow and soon left

away from the fence, with a blue bridleway arrow, to meet a lane. Go through a hedge gap and turn left on the lane which bends sharply left and heads towards **Caldecote Farm**. Immediately before the farm, turn sharp right on a track with a blue arrow and follow this as it bends left (ignore a much narrower path ahead). After half a mile, the track bends sharply right and heads for a lane. Turn left here and stay on the lane back into Oxborough, where you will see the Bedingfield Coach House across the green. (2¾ miles)

Across the Foulden road from the pub is the magnificent moated Oxburgh Hall, now a National Trust property, which has been the home of the Bedingfield family since Sir Edmund had licence to build in 1483 at the end of the Wars of the Roses. Immediately opposite the pub is the parish church of St John the Evangelist, semi-ruined since the tower and spire collapsed in 1948, destroying the nave roof. The beautiful 16th century Bedingfield Chapel escaped damage and boasts rare terracotta screens, among the earliest in England.

Date walk completed:

WARHAM, THE NORFOLK COAST PATH AND WELLS-NEXT-THE-SEA

THE BUSY HARBOUR AT WELLS-NEXT-THE-SEA

Distance:
10½ miles or
8 miles

Starting Point:
The Three
Horseshoes pub
(or overflow field
opposite).
GR 948417

Map: OS Landranger 132 or Explorer 251

How to get there: *Warham is 2 miles south-east of Wells-next-the-Sea, signed just off the road to Walsingham. Another option – and this would give you the 'best bit' of the walk at the end – would be to start in Wells, where there are several car parks, following the instructions from the Quay.*

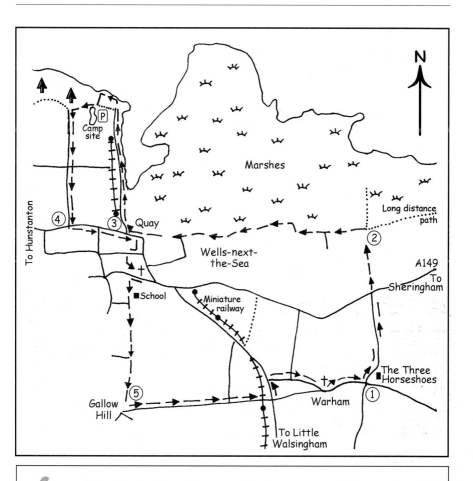

A peaceful flint-built village, a lively town with a colourful harbour, a delightful marshside stroll, a beach and even a couple of long views – this walk combines much of what is best in Norfolk's life and landscape. Warham is, strictly speaking, two villages – St Mary and All Saints – though usually known as one, and just up the road opposite the pub is one of the best examples of an Iron Age camp in England, probably an Iceni home. Wells-next-the-Sea is some way from it nowadays but has the charm of a slightly old-fashioned seaside resort with a network of narrow streets and alleyways.

The Three Horseshoes is an atmospheric 18th century pub caught in a time warp – stone floors, gas lighting and a longcase clock ticking away steadily. But there's nothing pretentious and bought-in-by-the-yard here; this is how it has been for donkey's years and it seems exactly right.

First mentioned in a 1725 will as an alehouse, possibly with a smithy on site, it was owned at one time by the Holkham Estate and became a freehouse in the 1960s. The interior – 'top bar' with scrubbed deal tables and high-backed settles, middle room like a Victorian parlour complete with faded portraits of royalty, and farmhouse kitchen-style end room – has a genuinely cosy atmosphere with friendly service to match.

The food, too, has a period feel, described by the owners as 'Mrs Beeton-style' with hearty, traditional dishes using local ingredients such as Stiffkey mussels and Wells crabs – and no chips. A range of homemade pies, including cranberry lamb, and beef and rabbit, is popular, as is the cheese-baked crab. Other dishes could include tomato braised pork chop, parsnip and butterbean bake and smoked mackerel hotpot, all served with a dish of well-presented vegetables.

Real ales *are Greene King IPA and Woodforde's Wherry, the latter served straight from the cask, plus a weekly guest. Whin Hill cider from Wells and a homemade lemonade are also on offer.*

There is an attractive beer garden and overnight accommodation in three

The Walk

① Turn right out of the pub car park and head along **Chapel Street**, passing traditional flint cottages, and out of the village on the quiet lane that becomes **Stiffkey Road** and climbs gently between hedges. Over to the left are occasional views across farmland to **Wells**. Cross the A149 coast road, keeping ahead on a pleasant track, and soon the sea comes into view in the distance across the saltmarsh. Go through a metal gate and turn left onto a broad, grassy path that is part of the **Norfolk Coast Path** extension to the Peddars Way. (1½ miles).

This is a truly wonderful place to be, and perhaps best of all on a sunny day in summer when the saltmarsh is tinged purple with drifts of sea-lavender, oystercatchers are dashing about overhead and small songbirds such as whitethroats and linnets perch on the tips of gorse bushes by the path. In the far distance the sea shimmers through the heat haze and there is a great feeling of peace and freedom. From here to Wells and then out to the sea, the path is a birdwatcher's delight and I would strongly recommend taking binoculars. In summer, graceful little terns can usually be seen plunging into the main channel between the harbour and the sea, and in winter the sky is alive with flocks of brent geese.

② Stay on the path as it skirts the marsh, for a short distance between trees and then with an acorn long-distance marker and yellow arrow along a bank that doglegs round an area of shallow pools popular with wading birds. There is then a channel of deeper water to the right before the path leads past a small boatyard on the left and the old whelkhouses on the right, where the smelly process of preparing locally-caught whelks for sale was carried out. Stay ahead as the path becomes a road heading towards the quay, past the old **Shipwrights Arms** pub, one of several in the town to have a plaque put up by the local history group to mark its previous life. Walk past the former grain warehouses, now converted to flats, on the left and then along the quay, very popular with holidaymakers but still a working area where crabs are landed in good numbers and a variety of other boats are moored. For the

THE 18TH CENTURY THREE HORSESHOES, WARHAM

shorter walk, turn left up **Staithe Street** (see point 4).

Crabs also provide the quarry here for the ancient sport of 'gillying', much loved by children (and quite a few adult 'helpers' too), in which bait – bacon and whelks are the most popular – is dangled over the edge of the quay on a long line and the small creatures foolish enough to cling to it are hauled out. The distance from the water can be several feet, depending on the tide, and it is a skill to land a crab in your bucket. Much too small to eat, they are thrown back at the end of each session – during the summer season some must go up and down scores of times.

Stay on the quay as it bends to the right, past the sea defence barrier that can be manoeuvred on rails across the road, then past the old maritime museum and out onto the grass and wildflower-covered embankment which runs alongside the main channel towards the sea. (2¼ miles)

On the other side of the beach road from the quay, apart from handily-placed public toilets, are a plaque at Liars Corner to John Fryer, who was the sailing master on HMS Bounty and cast adrift with Captain Bligh after the mutiny in 1789, and also a memorial to the 11 crewmen of the Wells

lifeboat Eliza Adams who lost their lives in an 1880 disaster. Here, too, is the start of the popular miniature railway that ferries holidaymakers out to the beach and Pinewoods camp site.

③ You can either walk on a surfaced path below the top of the bank, with fine views across the marshes, or along the ridge itself, where you also have a long view inland towards the **Holkham Estate**. At high tide the channel is busy with boats but at any time this is a pleasant and bracing stroll, eventually passing the large camp site on your left. At the end of the bank keep straight on, through a gap in the dunes, onto the main beach where you turn left past beach huts that have become much sought-after (and increasingly expensive). If the tide is right up – a fairly rare occurrence, it has to be said – a paddle to cool your aching feet will be easy now. After about 150 yards on the sand, turn left up the wooden steps of the first exit from the beach, immediately after the refreshment kiosk and before the splendidly-named **Wellzangelz** beach hut. Go down the steps at the other side and through the belt of pine trees planted along the coast for over three miles as a sea defence. This is also a well-known birdwatching area that has attracted many rarities over the years. Turn right at the foot of the steps, past the end of a lake and immediately left by a **Holkham**

Nature Reserve board onto an attractive reed-fringed path skirting the camp site. After about 400 yards turn left through a wooden gate and onto a broad track heading straight back towards Wells, with a tall hedge on the left and open farmland to the right. Soon there is open land on both sides where flocks of geese are a common sight in winter and away to the right can be seen the top of a monument in **Holkham Park**. (2 miles)

④ Eventually the track meets a road where you turn left back into Wells. Retrace your steps for a short distance past the quay and turn right immediately after the Golden Fleece pub up **Staithe Street**, a busy lane lined with a good range of shops and cafés. At the T-junction turn right on **Station Road** and immediately left into the **Buttlands**, a tree-fringed green flanked by handsome Georgian houses. Pass the Globe Inn and head down the left-hand side of the green, turning left at the bottom, by the Crown Hotel, onto an alleyway called **Chancery Lane**. Turn right on **High Street** and right again by the fine St Nicholas' church onto **Burnt Street**. Take the next road on the left, **Market Lane**, which leads past Alderman Peel High School, where

the gates are decorated with a motif of oars, to the cemetery. Turn left round the corner of the cemetery and ahead on a track that climbs gradually, soon joining a broader, stony track passing barns on the left. At the top of the slope, a point known as **Gallow Hill**, there is a crossroads of tracks where you turn left immediately before a house with a red-tiled roof and tall chimneys. (2¼ miles)

⑤ This is now a lovely hedged path along a ridge with fine views down to **Wells** and the sea, and occasional glimpses right towards **Walsingham**. The broad verges here were full of wildflowers as I passed in summer, with the purples of common mallow and field scabious prominent. Eventually the path leads past a fine group of old red-brick and tile barns on the left – unconverted as yet to holiday homes, though I dare say this will happen – and then down a slight slope to cross the line of the narrow-gauge **Wells and Walsingham Railway**. Keep ahead for 50 yards to the road, where you turn left for a short distance and then right, signed 'Warham', on the lane past flint cottages back into the village and the Three Horseshoes. (2½ miles)

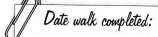

Date walk completed:

COLKIRK, OXWICK AND WHISSONSETT

ST MARY'S CHURCH, WHISSONSETT, AT THE FOOT OF THE CAMPINGLAND

Distance:
7½ miles

Map: OS Landranger 132 or Explorer 238

Starting Point:
The Crown pub.
GR 921264

How to get there: *Colkirk is 2 miles south of Fakenham, signed off the B1146 towards Dereham. Coming from Fakenham, the Crown pub is on the right in the village centre.*

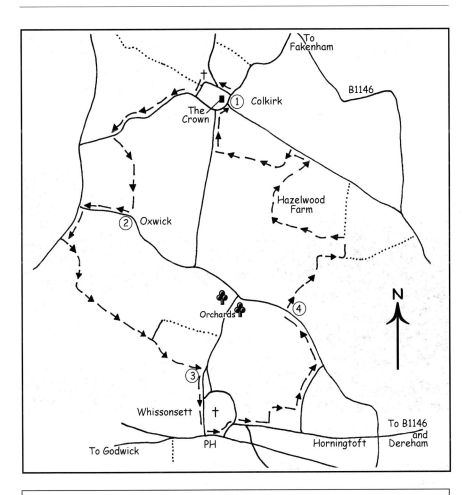

*W*alking in Norfolk is very much about walking through arable farmland, which is uninspiring if it is acres of sugar beet but much more attractive if fields of ripening barley rippling in the breeze. Even so, it's interesting to come across something rather more unusual, which this walk is likely to provide. The area around Whissonsett – which holds happy memories as my first proper Norfolk home – is well known for its apple orchards, soft fruit such as blackcurrants and a range of herbs including mint, parsley and tarragon. The walk also takes in a long and pleasant grassy track flanked by an ancient hedgerow.

The Crown is a traditionally-styled red-brick pub combining the roles of unspoilt local inn and restaurant serving a good range of homemade food. The building dates from the 17th century and has probably been a pub for most of that time, also having a butcher's shop on the premises in the early 19th century. Unusually, for several years after the Second World War it was owned by the village in the shape of the Trustees of the Poor of Colkirk, though whether the charity's handouts included free pints I cannot discover.

At the road end of the open-plan pub is a small, comfortable bar, then the handsome main bar with its red-tiled floor, high-backed wooden settles and exposed brickwork, with an airy no-smoking dining room beyond that. Outside is a pleasant patio area and a large beer garden on the old bowling green.

Fresh fish is well featured on the specials chalkboard, including panfried black bream, and salmon fillet with creamy lemon sauce, while among other dishes are fruity pork curry and baked cinnamon leg of duck with Cumberland sauce. Roast vegetable and goat's cheese bake is an example from a good veggie selection. A light lunchtime menu includes a range of baguettes and homemade soup.

Real ales *in this Greene King house are the brewery's IPA and Abbot Ale plus a guest such as Everards Tiger bitter. There are around 30 wines listed on a blackboard, most of them available by the glass.*
Telephone: 01328 862172.

 *The Walk*

The attractive village of Colkirk possibly takes its name from the Old Norse meaning Koli's church, one of several places in the area, including Horningtoft, to have its roots in the invasions from Scandinavia.

① Turn left out of the pub car park and head down **Crown Road**, which bends left to become **Church Road**. Where the main road bends right, keep ahead along the lane with the playing field on your right. The squat tower of **St Mary the Virgin** is just visible on the right behind a beautiful collection of trees. Opposite the church, turn left on **Gormans Lane** and, at the T-junction, right on **Raynham Road**. There are good views to the left now over farmland interspersed with copses typical of this part of Norfolk. Just after passing a farmhouse set back from the road on the left, where the road bends right, turn left onto a track with a footpath fingerpost. A sign here tells that the house has the splendid name of Duckwaddle Barn. After 300 yards, where the track bends left, turn right into the field and head left on a well-cut path between cropfields – golden barley on one side and wheat on the other as I passed. The path now runs alongside a hedge to the right and soon meets a lane, with the ruined **church of All Saints** just visible behind trees. (1¼ miles)

② Turn right on the lane and at the T-junction turn left on the road signed to **Tittleshall** and **Litcham**. After about 500 yards, turn left on a broad, grassy track along a field edge, with a hedge on your left. At the time of writing, the public footpath sign was missing here but I am hopeful it will be replaced. Follow the path as it bends right and then left, passing attractive meadowland where elegant swallows and house martins skimmed the tall grasses as I stopped for a breather. You stay straight ahead on this track for more than a mile now, ignoring paths off to the left and right, as it passes first between tall hedges and then has open farmland on the right with views over to fields planted with rows of soft fruit. When I lived in the area, this was my favourite place to walk our dog Bracken, who loved to chase up and down the track. I often admired the tall hedgerow here, which must be an ancient one judging by the number of different species in it – a joy to look at whatever the time of year. There is a good variety of birdlife here too,

yellowhammers being particularly noticeable. Eventually the track runs between hedges again to meet a lane. (2 miles)

③ Turn right on **London Street** into **Whissonsett**.

This quiet village off the beaten track appears in the Domesday Book as Witchingseta ('the fold of Wic's people') and its inhabitants have long been known for their strong and active community spirit. St Mary's church, built of flint and freestone, dates back to about 1250 though an Anglo-Saxon cross dug up in the churchyard and now displayed in the church suggests that Christian worship probably goes back much further here. The cross is thought to date from about AD 920 and could have been buried at the time of Danish raids in the area.

Stay on this road as it climbs gradually through the village, passing attractive cottages on both sides – sadly two shops here have closed in recent years – and the village hall on the left, behind which is the bowling green where for a while I was a moderately successful member of the B team. At the junction, turn left by the Swan pub onto **High Street**. (A detour here to the right – 2 miles in total – along the road to **Tittleshall**, would bring you to the deserted medieval village of **Godwick**, which declined during the 15th and 16th centuries for a variety of reasons and where the old street pattern can still be seen. The site can be visited from April to October.) Soon you pass the bus shelter on your left, which not only offers a welcoming bench but has a colourful children's mural showing the apple orchards, growing mainly Cox's Orange Pippins and Bramley Seedlings. Also on the left is **St Mary's church** in its delightful position at the bottom of the long stretch of grass known as the **Campingland**.

The village sign here pays tribute to the remarkable courage shown by Lt Col Derick Seagrim VC and Major Hugh Seagrim GC, the only brothers to win Britain's two highest awards for gallantry. Derick was awarded the Victoria Cross posthumously in 1943 after leading his men to capture an enemy machine-gun position during the Western Desert campaign and dying from fatal wounds two weeks later in another attack. Hugh took charge of a guerrilla mission in Burma, where he became a hero to the local Karen people as, wearing their costume, he led them on many raids against the invading Japanese. In March 1944, the Japanese sent a message that unless he surrendered they would kill one Karen for every day he was at large. He gave himself up and

was executed in September 1944. Hugh had clearly become a legend among the tribespeople who, because of his 6ft 4in height, gave him the nickname Hpu Taw Kaw, Grandfather Longlegs. When the sign was unveiled in 1985, representatives of the Karens joined villagers and dedicated a plaque there which reads: 'Grandfather Longlegs, we remembered so we came'.

Pass the post office, turn left on **New Road** and after 100 yards right onto a lane by a house called Sunset View, semi-derelict when I lived in the village but, happily, now restored. After passing **Church Farm** on the left and a row of modern houses called **Rectory Terrace** on the right, turn left after a further 50 yards onto a broad path with a fingerpost, along a field edge. After 100 yards, turn sharp right onto a path cut through a cropfield, following a yellow arrow marker. This leads straight across a second field to meet a narrow lane. Turn left and, shortly, at the T-junction, left again onto a wider lane. After about half a mile turn right onto a track with a fingerpost. (2 miles)

④ The track passes between cropfields which could well have in them one of the herbs grown locally – parsley when I was last there – then bends left and, shortly, right with yellow arrows. After 200 yards of grassy path you reach an area of concreted hard-standing. The map shows a footpath off to the left just before this but there is no sign of it on the ground so you turn left at the hard-standing onto an unsigned concrete track. After about 150 yards, turn left onto another unsigned concrete track between cropfields, which eventually bends sharp right immediately after a copse of tall poplar trees to pass **Hazelwood Farm** on the right. Keep ahead along the broad concrete driveway and when this meets a lane, turn left. After 200 yards turn left on a track with a bridleway fingerpost – the 'Private Road' sign here is aimed at drivers, not walkers. Soon pass farm buildings on the left and follow the track as it bends right, with a hedge on the right and good views over open farmland to your left.

There are in this area several stands of poplars growing, and the story I heard locally was that these are Lombardy poplars planted by farmers returning from service during the First World War in France, where these graceful trees had caught their eye.

Where the track meets a lane, turn right into Colkirk, turning right at the T-junction and following the road round left, back to the pub. (2¼ miles)

Date walk completed:

CASTON, BRECKLES HEATH AND THOMPSON COMMON

CASTON'S ATTRACTIVE VILLAGE SIGN

Distance:
11 miles or
6½ miles

Starting Point:
The Red Lion pub.
GR 961977

Map: OS Landranger 144 or Explorer 237

How to get there: *Caston is 4 miles south-east of Watton. Coming from that direction, turn left off the A1075, signed 'Stow Bedon', and keep straight ahead to Caston. The Red Lion pub is on the right at a junction next to the village green.*

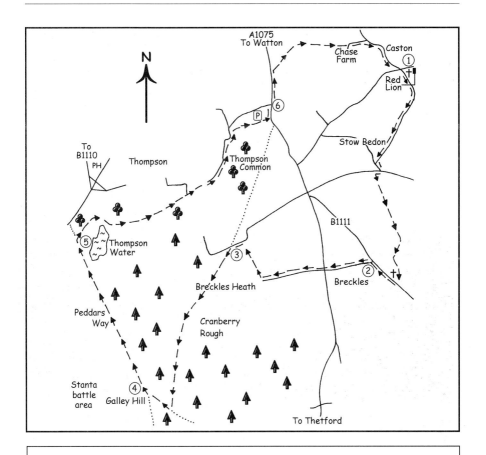

By the side of the Peddars Way near Thompson Water is a slate-slab sculpture on which are engraved the words: 'The footprints of our ancestors, familiar as our own faces, remote as fossils, written on clay and washed away, over and over.' It has the right ring to it for this varied walk, where you can stride out on the path of Roman soldiers and see the circular prehistoric pools known as pingos, formed after the Ice Age when circular discs of ice melted. Your adventure element could be either a glimpse of modern war games or the twisting trail over swampy Thompson Common, one of the most interesting areas of Norfolk. However, please note that because the common is a nature reserve, dogs cannot be taken on this walk unless you choose the short-cut option.

The Red Lion is a traditional flint and tile pub that has records of licences as far back as 1836, though it was more than likely a couple of farm cottages long before that. The owners now are aiming to mix the old with the new – reinstating a hitching rail for the use of local horseriders and putting in a cashpoint to save villagers a car journey.

Inside, the three smallish rooms are atmospheric – beams, whitewashed walls and red-tiled floors – with a non-smoking restaurant particularly attractive in dark red décor.

Food is a mixture of traditional and modern, a good range of chargrilled steaks alongside baked fillet of cod coated with pesto, and stir-fried sweet and sour chicken with a rice timbale. Veggie options include curried peanut loaf and three-cheese pasta and broccoli bake.

Real ales in this freehouse are Adnams Best Bitter and Greene King IPA with a guest such as Fuller's London Pride.
There is a pleasant beer garden to the side, and the pub is open all day Friday, Saturday and Sunday.
Telephone: 01953 488236.

 *The Walk*

① Turn left out of the pub car park and take the first lane on the left, passing the 14th century **church of the Holy Cross**. Stay on this narrow, quiet lane as it winds through attractive farmland with good views all round. Pass a lovely old flint house on the left, turn left at a T-junction and, after 100 yards, right on **Mere Road**. After a further 100 yards, turn left with a fingerpost on a path cut across the corner of a cropfield and veer right at the hedgeline. Soon the path bends left with a Norfolk County Council yellow arrow into a rough meadow, keeping close to a hedge on your right, then through a gap in a metal fence and ahead. At the next cropfield, the yellow arrow indicates straight ahead, though when I last did the walk this had been made difficult by lines of straw after harvest. If you can't go straight ahead, turn left and right to skirt the field, heading for a marker post at the far side. Now head diagonally right following a yellow arrow across the next cropfield – full marks to the farmer here as this was probably the best path cut through crops I have ever seen in Norfolk. The path bends left just before a hedge and now heads straight for **St Margaret's church, Breckles**. Go over a stile and follow the line of the churchyard wall round to the right then, at the corner, head diagonally right across the meadow to go through a wooden gate onto a road. Turn right here and soon pass the church. (2 miles)

St Margaret's is one of some 200 round-towered churches in Norfolk and Suffolk, though they are rare in the rest of the country. It used to be thought they were built this way because of a local shortage of large blocks of stone to form the corners of a square tower but the latest theory is that they are round for cultural reasons, many of them influenced by the Scandinavian invaders of East Anglia. Snakes carved on the inside of the tower

arch – built in AD 1000-1050 with the chequered flintwork top added in the 15th century – reflect styles found in Viking metalwork.

② After about 300 yards, immediately before the road bends left, turn left on an unsigned broad path along a field edge with a hedge on the right. Stay straight ahead as the main track bends right, soon following a yellow arrow marker, with farmland on the right, to meet the main road. Cross the A1075 and go straight ahead on a broad, unsigned track. In about half a mile, after ignoring paths to left and right, turn right into a belt of woodland following a public path fingerpost.

THE FRIENDLY RED LION PUB AT CASTON

This is now a lovely, shaded path between tall conifers, a good rest stop on a hot day. At a T-junction of paths, turn left to skirt the woodland, soon with open fields to the right, and follow a blue bridleway arrow to go through a wooden gate onto a broad track. Turn left and after 100 yards left again onto the **Great Eastern Pingo Trail**, whose footprint markers will now guide you for much of the way back. (1½ miles)

Alternatively, turn right here for the shorter walk and stay on the **Pingo Trail** to the car park at point 6, where you rejoin the main walk. (1 mile)

The trail now follows the line of the former Thetford-Swaffham rail line, known as the Crab and Winkle because it took so many holidaymakers to the North Norfolk resorts before closing in 1965. You have joined it where the old Crossing Keeper's Cottage stood.

③ Stay ahead now for a good mile on a very pleasant path which passes alternately through open farmland and woodland and is alive with butterflies such as meadow brown and speckled wood in summer. The woodland thickens as you pass **Cranberry Rough** on the left, a swampy wilderness that was once an ancient lake known as **Hockham Mere**. Where a broader track crosses your path, stay ahead and slightly to the right of the old rail track as it enters a cutting, and after another quarter of a mile you reach a metalled track near **Galley Hill**, where gallows did indeed stand. Turn right for a short distance to join the **Peddars Way**. (1¾ miles)

The Way was built by the Romans some time after AD 61 as part of measures to pacify the Iceni tribes following Boudica's revolt. Perhaps fitting then that this stretch runs alongside the huge Stanford Training Area (Stanta), known locally as the Battle Area, which was created during the Second World War by evacuating several villages and then shooting them to bits as target practice. It is still used for military manoeuvres, and you could hear firing off to your left.

④ After a few more yards fork right where there is a sign indicating Stanta access, as the **Peddars** becomes a broad gravel track leading at first through conifer woodland and then with open meadowland on the right. The path narrows and becomes grassier to pass the slate-slab sculpture and then glimpses of **Thompson Water** to the right through trees. (1¼ miles)

⑤ Now turn right with the **Pingo Trail** arrow once again and with a Stow Bedon 4 km fingerpost. You are now in the strange jungle-like world of **Thompson Common** but, before going ahead, it is well worth a short detour on the first path off to the right and through a wooden gate to the lake, manmade in 1847, where there is a lovely picnic spot. Retrace your steps to the main path and then bear right to another wooden gate with a **Pingo Trail** arrow and a notice about not taking dogs any further. The narrow path now twists and turns for a good distance through damp, primeval-looking woodland, with weed-covered ponds and a tangle of trees on both sides. An occasional fallen tree or creeper across the path adds to the tropical rainforest feel. At a T-junction of paths turn right, soon crossing a broad plank bridge to turn sharp left alongside a stream which you follow for several hundred yards. Eventually turn left on a wooden bridge over the stream, through a wooden gate and diagonally right across a meadow where you could meet the 'Flying Flock' of sheep (see Walk 1). At the end of the meadow stay ahead on a grassy path, which broadens into a track and then runs into a lane as it passes two houses on the left and stables on the right. The lane bends left by a wood-and-thatch cottage, sharp right and left again. Just before a road junction, turn right on a path with a **Pingo Trail** arrow into light woodland, through a wooden gate and right. The path bends left through a lovely area of heathland rich in wildflowers, including spotted orchids, and passing a large pingo (a circular pond created during the ice age) – though with a very variable water level – to the right. The path then twists through woodland, on a boardwalk and through a wooden gate into a car park. (2½ miles)

⑥ Turn left to the A1075, cross it and turn left alongside a busy stretch of road that cannot, sadly, be avoided as the old railway line is not walkable here. After about 600 yards turn right onto a path with a fingerpost and almost immediately veer slightly right and ahead along a field edge with a hedge on your left. This is now a pleasant, open path that bends to enter another field, now with the hedge on your right and the black tower of **Caston Mill** ahead. Go through a metal gate and ahead along a grazing meadow, through another gate at the end and onto the driveway of **Chase Farm**. Where this meets the road, turn right to pass the village hall and attractive houses back to the pub. (2 miles)

Date walk completed:

SOUTH LOPHAM, THE ANGLES WAY AND GARBOLDISHAM

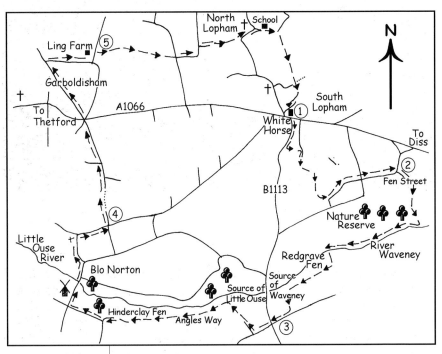

Distance:
11 miles

Starting Point:
The White Horse pub
GR 043815

Map: Landranger 144 or Explorer 230

How to get there: *South Lopham is 5 miles west of Diss on the A1066 to Thetford. The White Horse pub is on the main road in the village centre.*

A PEACEFUL POOL ON THE RIVER WAVENEY

*T*he 'adventure' of this walk lies in the fact that it crosses the county boundary into Suffolk which, I know, breaches the title of this book. But it would be a crying shame not to enjoy this beautiful stretch of the Angles Way, the 'Broads to Brecks' path running from Yarmouth to Knettishall Heath and so completing the Norfolk circle that starts with the Peddars Way. It takes in a splendid path close to the infant River Waveney, all reed-fringed tranquillity, offers a glimpse of the Little Ouse near its source and can also boast a couple of delightful green lanes across rolling South Norfolk farmland.

The White Horse is a pretty 16th century inn and its creeper-clad front hides a secret – it was extensively rebuilt after being strafed with machine-gun fire during the Second World War, though the pub's brochure, sadly, gives no clue as to how this happened. In recent years the village has been waging war of a different kind, against heavy traffic on the busy A1066 but there is little sign of a noise problem inside the pub with its wealth of light-wood beams, exposed brickwork and wooden floors.

The main bar, restaurant and small 'quiet room' dining area all have a welcoming atmosphere, while outside there is the contrast of a large beer garden with two patio areas, even an outdoor pool table.

Food on the set menus, plus specials chalkboard, is a mixture of traditional English – steak and kidney pudding, Norfolk prime bangers and mash – and more exotic dishes such as aubergine Niçoise and seafood platter of salmon and tuna bites, butterfly prawns and calamari. There is a good choice of hot filled baguettes as well as cold sandwiches, with a senior citizens' lunch Monday-Friday.

Real ales *in this freehouse are Adnams Best Bitter, Greene King IPA and Morland Old Speckled Hen plus, usually, one guest.*
Overnight accommodation is available in three ensuite rooms and the pub is open all day.
Telephone: 01379 687252.

The Walk

① Cross the main road, turn left and immediately right on **Redgrave Road**. After about 400 yards, immediately after a red-brick house on the left with an 1883 date, turn left through a wooden gate onto a narrow path with a fingerpost. This soon heads straight along a field edge with a ditch on the right. Where it meets a broader, grassy track turn right and stay ahead as this narrows to a path along a field edge. At the end of the field, go over a stile and follow the direction of a yellow Norfolk County Council arrow diagonally left across a meadow. At the far side, cross a ditch on a plank bridge and head up the next field with a wire fence and hedge on the right. Go over a stile at the top of the field, turn right through a hedge and ahead on a path close to the hedge – this was rather overgrown when I was last there. Go through a wooden gate with a yellow arrow and ahead across the top of another field. Cross over a plank bridge onto a clear path cut through a cropfield to meet the bend of a quiet lane. Turn left, soon passing a couple of attractive thatched houses and at the crossroads keep ahead on **Low Common**. To the right, across farmland, you can now see the woodland of **Great Fen**. (1½ miles)

② At the T-junction turn right with a fingerpost onto the broad track of **Silver Street**, and as this bends left to the last few houses, turn right alongside a wooden gate on a path that leads behind a bungalow. Soon this becomes a delightful grassy track with a plantation of young trees on the left and then thicker woodland as it passes the entrance to **Redgrave** and **Lopham Fen** on the right.

This is a National Nature Reserve, the largest remaining valley fen in England and the source of the River Waveney, which flows to the sea at Lowestoft. It is also home to the rare great raft spider, which has achieved near-legendary status among Norfolk naturalists and must be a striking sight, judging by its picture on South Lopham's village sign.

Stay ahead as the path crosses a plank bridge and over a stile with a yellow arrow. Cross another bridge and follow the path as it bends left between tall reed beds where the squeaky-scratchy song of sedge

THE WHITE HORSE INN, SOUTH LOPHAM

warblers can be heard. The path veers right to a wire fence which you cross on a stile with a yellow arrow. Now turn immediately right alongside the fence with one of the green Angles Way arrows that will guide you as far as the crossroads before **Thelnetham windmill**.

Go over a plank bridge with a handrail and stay ahead on another lovely stretch of path, with the river only a few feet to your left, hidden at first by reeds but coming into sight as the vegetation thins. The river marks the boundary between Norfolk and Suffolk, and at **Waveney Sluice** you cross the water into foreign territory. Otters can sometimes be seen in the deeper water beyond the pleasingly low-tech sluice, which was built to help keep the fen wet for wildlife. Follow the narrow path with its tricky tree roots as it bends right into light woodland. Where the trees give way to a tall bracken bank on the left and the river can be glimpsed to the right, there is another entrance to **Redgrave** and **Lopham Fen**.

This makes an ideal picnic stop – climb the stile on the right and only 50 yards or so ahead is a pool in the river where you can sit among wild mint in summertime and watch dragonflies dart above the water.

Back on the path, keep ahead into woodland then go through a metal gate with spring-loaded opening and turn left with a yellow arrow. The path now twists between trees with open fenland stretching away to the right. The grassy path eventually bends left, through two metal gates close together and ahead for 50 yards to a lane. (2 miles)

③ Turn right on the lane and at the crossroads keep ahead on **Hinderclay Road**. After 300 yards turn right onto a broad path, with a fingerpost, which skirts a large poultry farm, turning sharp left halfway round. Cross a stream on a bridge with a metal rail and go ahead into light woodland. The path bends right with a wire fence to the left and a grassy area to the right. Cross a track and stay ahead along a path with **Hinderclay Fen** to the right then over a stile and concrete bridge and across a meadow rich in wildflowers. Another stretch of light woodland follows and the path bends right and left before running into a track which veers left to meet the elbow of a lane. Turn right here and at the next crossroads right again to pass **Thelnetham mill**. The road soon crosses the Little Ouse and back into Norfolk. Follow the road as it bends left into **Blo Norton**, ignoring two lanes to the right.

A footpath I had hoped to take here, clearly marked on the map, is missing so follow **Church Lane** as it bends round to the left, past the church and turn right on **The Street**. Take the first turning left, after about 500 yards, onto a narrower lane with a walkable grass verge. (3 miles)

④ Ignore **Clay Hall Lane** to the right then, where the lane bends sharp left, keep ahead with a fingerpost on a grassy path that heads uphill to the skyline. Where this meets a lane, keep ahead for a few yards on a slip road to meet the A1066. Cross close to a lovely lily pond, turn left and immediately right into a stretch of old road used as a layby. After 20 yards turn right onto a grassy 'road used as path' through farmland, with a good view left to **Garboldisham** church tower. The path runs into a track past a house on the left, then you turn right for a few yards and right again on a lane heading uphill. After about 600 yards turn left at a junction of lanes, soon passing barns on the left. (2 miles)

⑤ Opposite **Ling Farm** house turn right on an unsigned grassy path with a long barn to the right. The path runs between hedges, past an isolated cottage and ends at a lane with a pillbox on the right. Go

straight forward on the lane, which bends sharp left and right, and you now have the rather oddly-shaped tower of **St Nicholas' church** at **North Lopham** ahead of you. Pass the hideous water tower and just before a road junction turn left into the churchyard. Go round the front of the church – which has some fine flintwork – and turn left on the road. Where this bends sharply left, turn right immediately before St Andrew's School on an unsigned track which soon becomes a lovely grassy path rich in flowers such as great willowherb. This is, in fact, **Primrose Lane**, though only at the other end will this become apparent; it is also something of a mystery as it is not properly marked on the map but is clearly well used by local people. Ignore a fork to the left and follow the path as it bends right, soon running between hedges then with open farmland on both sides. Keep ahead across a concrete pad and stay ahead as the path runs first into a track then a lane. At the T-junction turn left and left again back to the pub. (2½ miles)

Date walk completed:

WEST RUNTON, FELBRIGG HALL AND 'POPPYLAND'

FELBRIGG HALL, NOW IN THE CARE OF THE NATIONAL TRUST

Distance:
8¼ miles

Map: OS Landranger 133 or Explorer 252

Starting Point:
The Village Inn.
GR 181428

How to get there: *West Runton is 2 miles east of Sheringham on the A149 coast road. As you drive towards Cromer, the Village Inn is just after the church on the left, set back from the main road. The car park is signed on the left before the pub.*

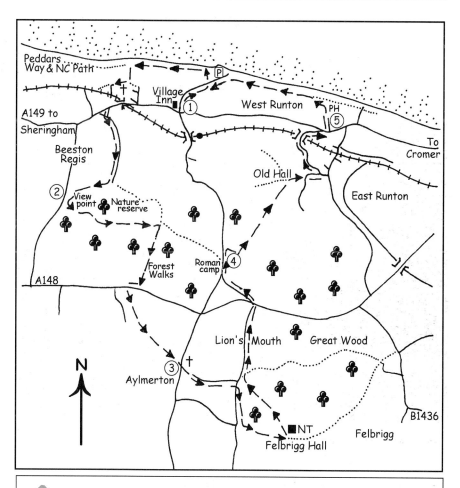

Peddars Way & NC Path
Village Inn ① West Runton PH ⑤
A149 to Sheringham
Beeston Regis
② View point · Nature reserve
A148
Forest Walks
Roman camp ④
Old Hall
East Runton
To Cromer
N
Aylmerton ③
Lion's Mouth   Great Wood
B1436
■ NT
Felbrigg Hall   Felbrigg

plendid sea views, attractive woodland paths and a dip into the beautiful parkland setting of Felbrigg Hall combine to make this a memorable walk. The many caravan sites in this area are, admittedly, rather hard on the eye but at least they don't block access to an excellent stretch of clifftop – near where the fossilised skeleton of a giant elephant was found – and you soon climb well above them into the highest part of Norfolk. Here, wooded hills and wildflower meadows – this part of North Norfolk has been given the name Poppyland – play their part in its designation as an Area of Outstanding Natural Beauty.

The Village Inn is one of the more unusual pub buildings in Norfolk, described as looking more like a bowls club pavilion behind its expanse of grassed beer garden. Mainly single-storeyed and flint-built in the early 20th century, it has leaded lights and a handsome dark-wood interior in the Edwardian style. It was originally a coach house for nearby Runton House and was later used as the clubhouse for a golf course. In the 1940s it became a pub with the fanciful name of Ye Yn of Runetune and was renamed the Village Inn by 1967.

There is a relaxed, comfortable atmosphere throughout the main bar with a non-smoking dining room off it, the cosy side bar and the large family room at the back, increased in winter by three log fires.

The food aims to be 'good-quality pub grub', most of it homemade with an emphasis on fish dishes and large salads. Griddled swordish, tuna steaks and red snapper may be found on the chalkboard menu, alongside Cromer crab, pan haggerty, chicken rogan josh and giant Yorkshire pudding with sausages. Mediterranean vegetable lasagne and vegetable korma are among a good veggie selection and there is a range of sandwiches and hot ciabattas.

Real ales *in this freehouse are Woodforde's Wherry, Bass and Hancock's HB and there are some 20 wines on the list, most available by the glass.*
A sunny terrace and walled beer garden offer pleasant places to rest after your walk and the pub opens long hours in summer.
Telephone: 01263 838000.

The Walk

① Turn left out of the car park to pass in front of the **Village Inn** and left onto **Water Lane**. The road veers right, signed to the beach, and immediately after a mini football pitch on the left you turn left through one of several unsigned gaps in the bank and head straight up the car park field to the high bank before the clifftop. Turn left at the entrance to Laburnum Caravan Park onto the permissive path along the cliff, keeping close to the wire fence and through a gap at the far end of the site. This is now a bracing (to put it mildly) stretch of the walk where a stiff breeze always seems to be blowing. Below you is the North Sea and ahead the geological quirk of **Beeston Bump**, which lays claim to being the highest point in Norfolk. The path runs close to the clifftop in places, so take care if there are children with you. Immediately before the next caravan site (Beeston Regis) turn left up the field, heading straight for **All Saints' church**. At the churchyard wall turn right into the caravan park and first left, which takes you to a crossing over the single-track railway line. Keep ahead for 20 yards to the main road, which you cross, and go through a gateway onto an unsigned track to the right of the entrance to Beeston Hall School. After a few yards the track bends slightly left with a yellow Norfolk County Council arrow and a long-distance path acorn marker to pass **Hall Farm** and a lovely flint cottage, due to open as a tearoom with walkers in mind in 2003. The broad, sandy track heads up a steepish slope between bracken banks to a junction of paths by woodland. Turn right

here with a public bridleway fingerpost and after 20 yards pass in front of a part-thatched cottage. The path narrows to run alongside woodland with views to the sea on the right as you ignore a path to the left with a horseshoe marker.
(2 miles)

② Immediately before a house, where a broad track comes in from the right, turn left up a narrow path where there is a National Trust Beeston Regis Heath sign. The path climbs steeply to a wooden bench where you can catch your breath with a superb view laid out below you – to the left **Sheringham** and the coast stretching away towards

THE VILLAGE INN AT WEST RUNTON

Blakeney Point, with **West** and **East Runton** to the right. Keep ahead between the bench and a trig point on a path that bends left through light woodland. At a T-junction of paths turn right with an NT horseshoe marker and after 10 yards left, still with the horseshoe. There now follows a delightful stretch of woodland walk but tricky in that it leads though a network of unsigned paths. You need to keep more or less straight ahead, sometimes slightly left or right of centre, ignoring all paths off to the sides for about half a mile (horse-droppings help to indicate you are on the bridleway) until you reach a T-junction with a broader track. Turn right here and in a short distance right again at the next T-junction. This leads to the edge of the wood where you keep straight ahead, with a yellow arrow, through a gap in the hedge and on a clear path across a cropfield. This path meets the busy A148, where you turn right on the grass verge past Woodlands guesthouse. After 100 yards turn left across the road, over a stile by **Home Farm** and across a narrow meadow. Go over another stile and ahead across a cropfield on a path that may not be too clearly cut but leads to a hedge at the far side. Turn left here and after 30 yards right through a gap in the hedge with a yellow arrow. You now head diagonally left on paths across three more cropfields, aiming straight for a church tower. (1¾ miles)

③ You emerge onto a lane opposite the fine round-towered **church of St John the Baptist, Aylmerton**, where you turn right and then left between the church and Old House on a pleasant, broad track across farmland. This meets a lane by a Dutch-gabled house dated 1864, standing at an entrance to **Felbrigg Park**. Turn right on the narrow, shady lane and immediately before a road junction turn left with a public footpath fingerpost through a metal gate into the park. The path winds more or less straight ahead across parkland with mature trees, soon with a red Felbrigg trail arrow on a low post. After a further 100 yards turn left with the red arrow through a wooden gate into woodland. When this path meets a broad, gravelled drive, turn right through a gate alongside a cattle grid, now with a **Weavers Way** marker, up to the magnificent frontage of **Felbrigg Hall**, where there is good shade under trees for a rest stop.

Felbrigg, run by the National Trust, is one of the finest 17th century houses in East Anglia. It had a major internal refit in the 1750s but was untouched by Victorian modernisation. Entrance to the beautiful grounds is free to walkers and cyclists and there is a tearoom (phone 01263 837444 for opening hours).

Retrace your steps to the gate and

keep ahead on the driveway, over a cattle grid to meet the lane by the house you saw earlier. Turn right on the lane, known as the **Lion's Mouth** as it climbs gradually through a stretch of woodland with huge old trees. Where it bends right to meet the A148, turn left up the bank to meet the road, left again for a few yards and cross onto a lane with a 'No Entry' sign for traffic. Follow this lane for about half a mile, past a water tower on the right and keeping ahead, signed '**West Runton**', at a road junction. (2 miles)

④ Opposite a National Trust sign for Roman Camp and Caravan Park, turn right and keep ahead on a path with a public footpath fingerpost and green circular walks arrow, ignoring a broad track to the left with an acorn marker. The narrow path leads steeply downhill through dense, jungle-like woodland to emerge into a lovely meadow full of wildflowers. Head across the field with a caravan park to your left and cross the long-distance **Norfolk Coast Path**, keeping ahead on a path with a public bridleway fingerpost. The sunken path between banks leads into a meadow full of poppies in season and then, at the next junction

of paths, turn right between over-arching hedges, passing a large flint-built house on the left to meet a lane at **East Runton**. Turn left and after 100 yards, opposite a playground, left again on **Buxton Close** (leading to **Brick Lane**). This lane passes houses and The Poplars Caravan Park to become a pleasant hedged track and soon you turn right on a bridge over the railway line. The path bends right, passing The Forge and continuing downhill to meet the A149. (1¼ miles)

⑤ Cross and keep ahead on a path with a yellow arrow alongside caravans. There is a long view now to the right towards **Cromer** parish church and pier, with its theatre and lifeboat station at the end. The path bends left to run along the clifftop, eventually leaving the caravans behind and skirting farmland – as earlier in the walk coming close to the cliff-edge at times. After an invigorating stretch with soaring seabirds to keep you company, the path meets the slipway at **West Runton**, where you turn left (avoid a stretch of road by turning into the car park and heading left up the long field) and retrace your steps to the pub. (1¼ miles)

Date walk completed:

ITTERINGHAM, CORPUSTY AND MANNINGTON HALL

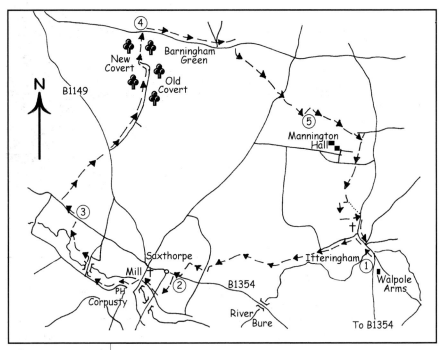

Distance:
9½ miles

Map: OS Landranger 133 or Explorer 252

Starting Point:
The Walpole Arms
pub.
GR 147306

How to get there: *Itteringham is 4 miles north-west of Aylsham, signed right off the B1354 from that direction. The Walpole Arms stands on the right just before you enter the village, at a junction of lanes.*

MEDIEVAL MANNINGTON HALL

*T*his walk crosses one of the quietest, least developed parts of Norfolk where it sometimes seems as though you have entered a wormhole through time. The lanes carry as little traffic as any in the county and the villages sleep on, regardless of the world outside. Even Corpusty, which was the exception to the norm, has benefited hugely from a recent bypass to regain its old tranquil atmosphere. There is a good variety of landscape here, too, from rolling arable farmland to flower-rich woodland and sheep pasture, and behind it all lies the historical legacy of one of England's great families, the Walpoles.

63

The Walpole Arms is an atmospheric and award-winning 18th century pub in a peaceful spot just outside Itteringham, a successful combination of traditional village inn and fine-food restaurant. The main bar is cosy, heavily beamed with stripped brick walls, timber posts dividing the room into smaller areas and a large, brick-built open fireplace. The 40-seater restaurant is more formal but still with the welcoming feel of a country dining room.

Two distinct menus reflect the aims. One is Mediterranean-influenced with such dishes as saltimbocca of pork with apple mash and broccoli; spinach, goat's cheese and pine nut pastie; and grilled sardines on toasted ciabatta.

The other 'brunch menu' is simpler and popular with walkers. It offers traditional dishes such as gammon, egg and chips, and chicken and ham pie alongside cockles or prawns with brown bread and more adventurous lighter bites including green beans, gorgonzola, pickled fig and hazelnut salad. There is also a good range of sandwiches. Walkers may phone the pub with orders, with an estimated arrival time, and the food will be ready for them.

Real ales served are Walpole Arms bitter, brewed by Woodforde's at Woodbastwick in the Broads, and a range from Adnams of Southwold – Best Bitter, Regatta and the stronger Broadside. An unusually long wine list has 46 entries plus nine half-bottles and house wines by the glass.
Food is served daily except Sunday evenings in winter; booking is advised for evening meals.
Outside there are pleasant beer gardens to the front and back.
Telephone: 01263 587258.

The Walk

Itteringham's peaceful atmosphere seems to belong to times long past. St Mary's church has stood above the slow-moving River Bure for 600 years and its interior is noted for the rich Jacobean panelling from a neighbouring house belonging to the Walpole family, whose most illustrious member was Sir Robert, Britain's first Prime Minister.

① Turn left out of the pub car park and keep straight ahead on the lane into the village, soon crossing over the **River Bure**. Just before **St Mary's church**, turn left on a track past the Bure Valley Community Centre. Head steadily uphill, ignoring a path to the right, and then down again, staying ahead on a path into damp woodland where the main track bends left. The going can be slightly tricky here along the muddy path but you may well be rewarded by the sight of a grey heron flapping clumsily away from the jungle to your left. At a T-junction of paths turn left with a yellow arrow and, when the path emerges from the wood, keep straight ahead across the cropfield to another marker. Now stay ahead with a hedge bank on your left, ignore a track to the left and at the next yellow marker head diagonally left across the field towards a clump of trees and telegraph poles, aiming to the left of a church tower just visible above the skyline. Keep ahead at the next yellow arrow and the path cuts through a grass bank to a broad track. Now turn left with a blue arrow and, after 200 yards, right. At the field's end turn left following an 'official path diversion' sign to meet the B1354. (2 miles)

② Turn right on the road and, just before the roundabout, left on to a track with the new bypass below to your right. Turn right over a stile and descend to the bypass, which you cross on a footpath which becomes a lane between houses. Turn left at the road by the Old Bakehouse then veer right on a narrow path to the right of the mill which leads to **Corpusty** village green.

Corpusty and Saxthorpe are twin villages separated only by the River Bure and they share a sign, a 100-year-old beam-type plough on

THE WALPOLE ARMS, ITTERINGHAM

whose base is the Ploughman's Prayer: 'The King he governs all; the Parson pray for all; the Lawyer plead for all; the Ploughman pay for all and feed all.' Both villages also shared in the wealth of Norfolk's medieval wool trade, with several mills involved in the industry. There are 38 names on the First World War memorial in the church, from a population at the time of 600 – said to be a higher percentage than any other village in England.

Cross the green to the Duke's Head pub, where auctions were held in Victorian times.

In 1886 the headmaster of the village school noted that 41 of his pupils were absent. He found they were playing truant to attend the auction and remarked that 'such little ones can have no business in such places'.

Turn right along **The Street**, passing a Victorian post box set into the wall and then a children's playground. The quiet cottage-lined lane bends right, past Wheatsheaf Nursery on the left. After 200 yards turn right onto **The Street** (Little London), soon crossing the **River Bure**. Opposite a track leading off to the right, turn left over a stile with a yellow footpath arrow, cross the field to another stile and turn left, following the path as it curves round

the field edge. Red-legged partridges scurry ahead and blackthorn brightens the hedge in season as the path leads up a bank to the road. (1¾ miles)

③ Turn left along the road and, after reaching the brow of a slope, turn right onto a footpath with a fingerpost and yellow marker. Keep straight ahead along the field edge, ignoring a path to the right but keeping an eye out for hares bounding across to your left, until you reach the B1149. Cross the road and continue ahead along a track with a fingerpost towards **Shrubbs Farm**. Pass farm buildings and then a cottage on the right before entering the attractive woodland of **Old Covert** and **New Covert**. As might be expected from these names, there are pheasants here – we saw guinea fowl too – and rhododendrons flower in late May/early June. Grassy banks make this a good rest stop. The track heads downhill through the wood then, with open country on the right, bends to the left. After 150 yards, immediately after a wooden hut, turn right on a lovely unsigned path that leads uphill alongside mature conifers on your left with more open birch scrub on the right, to meet a narrow, shady lane. (2¼ miles)

④ Turn right on the lane, soon leaving the woodland behind and heading into open farmland with big skies all around. Opposite **Green**

Farm, a handsome brick and flint house with fine chimneys, turn right onto a path with a barn on your left and, after 100 yards, bear diagonally left following a Norfolk County Council circular walks marker. The path runs to the left of a low, grass bank, at the end of which keep ahead across a field to another marker and continue ahead, now to the right of a bank. Cross a lane and, following a fingerpost, head diagonally right across the corner of a field to a yellow arrow marker and turn left along a broad swathe of grass – another good picnic spot. (1¾ miles)

⑤ Soon turn left in front of a small wood, following a marker and heading for a stile. Turn right immediately before the stile along a path with a fence on your left and a woodland stream to the right. Go over a stile and the path bends right, across the stream to another stile. Now keep ahead along a pleasant green lane following a yellow arrow and ignoring a white-arrowed path to the right, which is part of the **Mannington Hall** estate trails. After another stile, turn right at the end of the field keeping woodland on your left, and the Hall with its lake can soon be seen to the right. Dogs must be kept on leads here, as the field is often full of sheep. Cross the lane, going over a stile and ahead along the pasture, but before doing so it is

worth taking a short detour to the right for a look at the front of the Hall.

Mannington Hall is a medieval moated manor house which has been, since 1735, in the Walpole family. Nearby Wolterton Hall was built for Sir Robert's younger brother Horatio, also a politician. Mannington is well known for its gardens, especially thousands of classic varieties of roses, many of them in areas designed in the 15th century.

As you approach the end of the long field, head diagonally right to its bottom corner and turn left over a stile with a yellow arrow marker. The path, edged with primroses and flag irises in season, heads through woodland with a stream on the right. At a junction of paths, turn left on a wooden bridge over a stream and up the field edge to meet a lane. Turn right into **Itteringham**, with its occasional advertising sign from another era, and soon pass **St Mary's church** to retrace your steps back to the **Walpole Arms**, sitting unostentatiously at a junction of lanes. (1¾ miles)

Date walk completed:

MARSHAM AND THE BURE VALLEY RAILWAY

THE BURE VALLEY RAILWAY RUNS ALONG PART OF THE WALK

Distance:
9¼ miles

Starting Point:
The Plough Inn.
GR 197243

Map: OS Landranger 133, 134 or Explorer 238 & Outdoor Leisure 40

How to get there: *Marsham is 2 miles south of Aylsham on the A140. As you enter the village, heading towards Norwich, the Plough Inn is on the right, set back a few yards from the main road.*

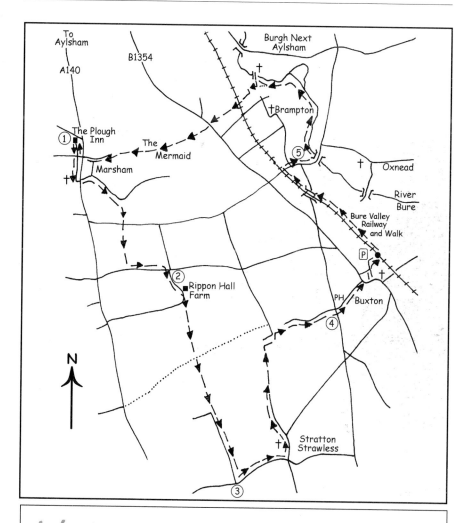

Within its nine and a bit miles, this walk combines much of what visitors to Norfolk find so appealing – after leaving behind the noise and hassle of one of the main roads bringing them here. Gently rolling farmland, narrow lanes with little traffic, an attractive church in a quiet village and a tranquil river that meanders through lush water meadows are all on offer. There is also the added bonus of a look at the narrow-gauge Bure Valley Railway and a good stretch of undeveloped grassland that is not too common in the county.

The Plough Inn is a substantial 18th century building that has had something of a chequered career, including a spell in the 1990s when it was renamed the Flags. Happily it is now close to having its traditional name back, as earliest references are to the Plough and Shuttle. Having begun life as a private house, the present building has also been tearooms, a farm produce shop, even a residential home for the elderly. It deserves a straight furrow now as it is an attractive inn with a friendly welcome and a good range of home-cooked food served in generous portions. Its main bar and restaurant are traditionally styled and well furnished – with a collection of gleaming copper, wooden dressers and spindle-backed chairs.

Food, too, is largely traditional. Homemade pies are a house speciality – Farmer's Pride with locally-supplied beef, Poacher's Delight with local game, and the vegetarian Crazy Carrot among them. Other dishes include a range of steaks, beef or Thai chicken stir-fry and baked sea bass, and among several veggie options is a casserole with herb dumplings. Lighter lunchtime specials and sandwiches are also available.

The Real Ale *on offer in this freehouse is either Woodforde's Wherry or Adnams Best Bitter. The policy is to keep just one real ale but keep it well. There is a pleasant beer garden at the front, and the Plough offers overnight accommodation in 13 rooms.*
Telephone: 01263 735000.

The Walk

① Turn right out of the car park and right again to pass in front of the pub on the **Old Norwich Road** parallel to the A140. Cross **High Street** and keep ahead, passing a large garage on the right. About 25 yards before the lane runs out, turn left with a public bridleway fingerpost to cross the main road and continue on a grassy track between banks. Stay ahead as the track broadens and opens out with cropfields on both sides. Where the main track bends sharply left, keep ahead following a blue Norfolk County Council bridleway arrow on a grassy path between hedges. This leads up a slope and broadens before meeting a lane, which you cross, staying ahead with a public footpath fingerpost. The path between tall hedges is heavily shaded at first but soon the hedges thin to give good views across farmland. When the path meets a lane, turn left and after about 500 yards, just after passing brick cottages and a lane on the left, turn right at **Rippon Hall Farm** onto a broad track that is part of the national farm walks scheme. (1½ miles)

② Stay on this sandy track as it bends right, between farm buildings and a handsome red-brick house. Keep ahead, across a narrow track, onto a long, straight stretch with hedges on both sides. This leads to a junction of tracks where you keep straight on, through a wooden gate with a yellow arrow marker and into attractive meadowland. Go through a metal gate and the path climbs to run along a field edge with extensive pasture to the right. Pass **Strattonhill Farm** on the right and the path broadens into a straight, flinty track.

Pass the lovely thatched Manor Cottage to meet a road. (1½ miles)

③ Turn left into **Stratton Strawless**, soon passing the village hall and sign. Follow **Church Road** round to the left, signed 'Buxton', to pass **St Margaret's church**.

The first part of the village name means 'settlement by a (Roman) road' and the second is probably no more complicated than simply 'without straw', though why is unclear. When I was here last, St Margaret's had a sign outside saying 'Lovely Church Open' and it is well worth a look. The low tower

THE ATTRACTIVE PLOUGH INN, MARSHAM

has a stone statue at each corner and, inside, an alabaster memorial from 1638 to landowner Thomas Marsham is the earliest in Norfolk to represent the Resurrection, showing him about to throw off his coffin shroud. Also buried here is Robert Marsham, a noted 18th century naturalist who planted more than two million trees.

Where the road bends sharply right, keep straight ahead on a broad track with a public bridleway fingerpost. This rather dull stretch of hedged track soon becomes narrower and more attractive, bending to pass a pond off to the left. Go through a wooden gate with a fingerpost and head straight across a meadow on a path that is not clearly defined but leads towards a second gate.

You are now quite close to RAF Coltishall and could well see, as I did, Jaguars flying an impressive formation. I much preferred to watch the aerobatics of a sparrowhawk circling above my head at exactly the same time as the planes roared by, but then maybe it was only in the air looking for small birds startled by the jets. It's an ill wind etc etc.

Go through the gate and ahead on a path between tall hedges, then through a metal gate and past a fine old barn on the right. The path bends sharply right then left and after 50 yards, at a junction of paths, turn right with a public footpath fingerpost. The broad path heads down a slope, alongside a metal gate and ahead on what is now a metalled track, passing Dudwick Cottage on the left and the large Dudwick House to the right. After a couple of cattle grids, the track crosses a stretch of parkland dotted with fine old trees, then by another grid to meet the road at **Buxton**. (2 miles)

④ Cross the road, passing the Black Lion pub (no food but you are welcome to eat your own sandwiches, closed Wednesdays) onto **Crown Road**. Stay ahead past the Crown pub, ignoring a road to Aylsham to the left, and after 150 yards turn left on **Stracey Road**. At the T-junction turn right into the **Bure Valley Walk** car park. Cross the line of the narrow-gauge railway – which runs for nine miles from Aylsham to Wroxham – and turn left onto a pleasant path, popular with walkers, cyclists and butterflies, that runs alongside the track. The path goes over a road as the rail line splits into two for a short section then back into single-track. Immediately before **Brampton** station platform (think miniature railway for size), turn right down a flight of steps to meet a lane, where you turn left. After 50 yards, just past a row of cottages, veer right as the main road bends left and pass the village sign using the old name Bramtuna (the two fishes on it are, presumably, a joke). At the next junction keep ahead, signed 'Tuttington', on a lane leading to a bridge over the **River Bure**. (2 miles)

⑤ Immediately before the bridge, squeeze through a gap to your left, with a yellow arrow, down over a stile and ahead along the riverbank. The path is not wonderfully well defined, but stays close to the river for a good distance now – a delightful stretch of the slow-flowing **Bure**, rich in birdlife and with water meadows on both sides. The path leads over a double stile, then another stile and into a wooded stretch that has overhanging branches. Though cut regularly, the riverside vegetation, including a stunning array of orange balsam in season, grows so quickly that the going can be quite difficult, and boggy in patches. Press on, over a wooden footbridge, and the path becomes easier, bending left as the river splits. Soon the path becomes a broad, grassy swathe that follows the river as it bends sharply left with a white-painted mill across the water. Stay by the river until you reach a gated wooden bridge on your right, which leads over to **Burgh next Aylsham church**. Turn left at the bridge, away from the river, and after 200 yards turn right with a yellow arrow through a wooden gate and over a bridge into a meadow with a stream on your left. After a further 50 yards, turn left on a concrete

bridge over the water and then right, soon passing under an old railway bridge. The stream narrows and is filled with watercress for a stretch before you go over a stile and along a field edge. At a lane, turn left for 10 yards and then right over a stile with a fingerpost on a path that is not too clearly defined but heads across attractive rough grassland, keeping close to the pretty stream, with its wonderful name of **The Mermaid**. At a small stone bridge, the path veers left away from the water for a few yards then right to run parallel again. Soon it heads diagonally left away from the stream to meet a hedgeline, where you turn right. Keep the hedge on your left for a short distance then veer right towards a post with a yellow marker. Go over a stile and the path meanders ahead, twisting right and left, across the next meadow, through a hedge gap and along the next field keeping close to the hedge. At the end of the field, turn right alongside a hedge and then ahead through a clump of trees. Eventually the path leads over a stile alongside a metal gate and onto a concrete track, passing large barns on the left to meet the main road. Cross onto the **Old Norwich Road** and turn right to the pub. (2¼ miles)

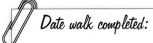

Date walk completed:

73

HONINGHAM, THE RIVER TUD AND MATTISHALL

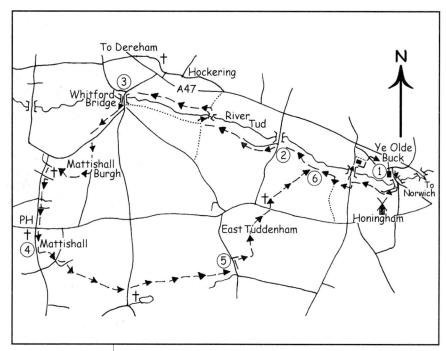

Distance:
8½ miles

Map: OS Landranger 133 or Explorer 238

Starting Point:
Ye Olde Buck Inn.
GR 103118

How to get there: *Honingham is 7 miles north-west of Norwich, signed just off the A47. Ye Olde Buck Inn is on a bend in the centre of the village.*

MATTISHALL VILLAGE SIGN, SHOWING NOSEY PARKER

It always gives me a lift – perhaps slightly malicious – during a walk if I catch sight of a busy road in the distance with traffic hammering past and I can think how lucky I am to be striding along in the fresh air. So it is here with arguably the least pleasant road in Norfolk, the A47, glimpsed as the path crosses lovely water meadows. The countryside round about is not as well known as many other parts of the county but there is a good variety of riverside walking, woodland and grassy pathways. Honingham is an attractive village to begin a walk, and Mattishall, halfway round, has a range of historic buildings clustered around the church.

Ye Olde Buck Inn is an attractive, white-painted pub, where the buck in question is not the expected animal but old John Buck, a notorious 18th century booze smuggler. Originally called the Bell and perhaps as old as 400 years, it was renamed when he was granted the pub's first alehouse licence in 1789. He is referred to in James Woodforde's *The Diary of a Country Parson* as 'Moonshine Buck', supplying him with a 'tub of cogniac brandy' for £1 18 shillings.

There is a friendly welcome and a comfortable feel to the heavily beamed main bar with its plaster walls, and the three smaller non-smoking restaurant rooms off to the sides. The emphasis is strongly on food, with a large range of traditional and foreign dishes on the regular menu and daily specials board. Should you have a favourite dish that doesn't appear, they will make it for you if they have the ingredients.

The standard (amusingly illustrated) menu includes such dishes as baked lamb with mint and feta; tenderloin of pork satay; and smoked haddock, cod and salmon crumble. Specials could feature asparagus ravioli with avocado and roasted red pepper, or halibut fillet on wild mushroom and courgette stir-fry. Good sandwiches are also available.

Real ales *are Adnams Best and Flowers Original and there is a large, pleasant beer garden.*
Telephone: 01603 880393.

The Walk

① Turn right out of the car park, passing in front of the pub. Go over the **River Tud** and, after 100 yards, turn right on Mill Lane following a yellow Norfolk County Council arrow. The lane soon becomes a track passing between hedges, over a stile, across a meadow and into light woodland alive with the song of birds, including the lovely, descending trill of a newly-arrived willow warbler as I passed. Reaching

a road, turn left and after 50 yards right over a stile by a metal gate with a footpath fingerpost. Skirt the left-hand edge of the field, close to woodland, and go through a metal gate at the end. Cross the narrow field to yellow markers, turn right alongside the hedge and then left at the field's end through a metal gate into a long, pleasant meadow. The A47 is away to your right as you pass a copse of graceful poplars, then continue through a metal gate and ahead, ignoring a green-arrowed path to your left. The path twists through a small wood, between gateposts then bending right on a wooden bridge over a ditch and left along the water meadow, staying close to the ditch. Pass a seat by a small pond and at the end of the meadow veer left and immediately right on a narrow path between trees. (1½ miles)

② At the lane turn left and soon right onto **Rotten Row**, passing cottages as fields rise to the skyline on your left. Keep ahead through **Riverside Farm** and onto a grassy path between fields, through a gap in the hedge and across another field. Now cross a ditch on a plank bridge, go over a stile and head diagonally

right across the field corner to a bridge with double stile. Climb these and continue straight ahead across the damp meadow, on a wooden bridge over the **Tud** and ahead to a yellow arrow. Turn left along the field edge, keeping the hedge on your right. Don't be too alarmed by the old 'Beware of Bull' sign on a gatepost – there is no evidence of the animal anywhere about – and keep straight ahead along the meadow as the path becomes broader and raised, with the river twisting away to your left. Pass through a metal gate and stay ahead, soon with a hedge on the right. At the end of the field turn left (unsigned) and then right at

YE OLDE BUCK INN TAKES ITS NAME FROM AN 18TH CENTURY SMUGGLER

the river on a wooden bridge. The path now leads across several bridges and railway-sleeper walks with yellow markers, passing through woodland close to the river. Turn right over a stile to meet the lane at **Whitford Bridge**. (1¾ miles).

③ Turn left along the lane which bends right after 200 yards; ignore a lane off to the left. The road climbs gradually between banks that are flower-studded in season, and soon the square tower of **St Peter's** at **Mattishall Burgh** comes into view ahead. Where the lane bends right, turn left onto a footpath signed with a yellow arrow, along the edge of a cropfield. Soon a second church can be seen on the right – the lantern spire of **All Saints'** at **Mattishall**. Keep straight ahead, now with a green circular walks marker as the path becomes more clearly defined and then leads along a broad, grassy strip with a hedge on the right. Keep ahead at the next green marker on a clear path through a cropfield and onto a broad track. After 20 yards turn right, still with the green arrow, across the field heading for the church. Turn left and right at the field end, over a stile and to **St Peter's** with its chess-piece tower. Turn into the churchyard and out at the far end, turning right into a lane. At the T-junction, turn left into **Mattishall**, passing modern bungalows and then the cemetery on the right. At the junction with **Norwich Road**, cross

and keep ahead but just to the right is the **Swan pub** if you're needing refreshment by this stage. (1½ miles)

Surrounded by Georgian houses, All Saints' on your right is an impressive church dating in part from the 14th century with a handsome tower topped by a spirelet. The drum-shaped village sign by the entrance to the churchyard caused something of an outcry when it went up in its specially constructed niche, some people thinking the glass-fibre material vulgar. It shows various spellings of the village name since it appeared in the Domesday Book as Mateshala, and it features prominently the original Nosey Parker – the Norwich-born Archbishop of Canterbury Matthew Parker, whose close watch on his clergy earned him the nickname and who married Mattishall woman Margaret Harlestone. Also depicted is a mule team led by a local dealer, or 'brogger', in the lucrative wool trade that was the basis of the village's prosperity.

④ Pass a range of attractive cottages on the left and immediately before a street on the left called **The Oaks**, turn left over a stile with a footpath fingerpost, passing a renovated mill tower, then go over another stile and ahead along the field edge. The path bends right, over a stile and ahead on a path through a cropfield. Cross a lane and continue ahead on a track with a fingerpost; where this bends left, veer right alongside a wooden gate on a grassy path with a small pond on your left. The path bends right across a field and then left on a broad, grassy strip that makes a good resting place. Stay ahead with a green arrow, ignoring a path to the right, and turn right and left into a small wood carpeted with primroses in spring. Turn right and left alongside a ditch, across a lane and onto a track following a fingerpost. This is now a pleasant grassy way popular with butterflies and with rolling, wooded countryside all around. Just after you pass a small wood on the right, a green arrow points directly ahead across a cropfield. (It could be that only a narrow channel has been left through the crops; if so, curse and divert anti-clockwise around the field edge.) Turn left at the hedge and immediately right alongside the field where the path is clearer. The path soon bends left and right to lead you through an unusual sliding pole gate then a metal gate, passing stables and a pink-washed house to a lane. (1¾ miles)

⑤ Now turn left on the lane and after 200 yards right onto a track with a green arrow, which soon becomes a grassy path along a field edge. At the field's end turn left, over a stile, bearing left around a field, then left and right onto the road. Turn right here then immediately left over a stile and straight ahead – the angle of the fingerpost is misleading – across the meadow with **All Saints' church, East Tuddenham**, to your left. The clear path stays close to the stream on your right then heads along a field edge. At the bottom, turn right across the stream on an earth bridge and then left heading for a metal gate. (1 mile)

⑥ Turn right through the gate and onto a path through the long meadow you covered earlier. Turn right at the end, left to the metal gate and up the right-hand field edge. Turn left along the lane, passing the path where you emerged near the start of the walk. Immediately after crossing the river there is a signed conservation walk to the right, with a map, which diverts from the OS map but is worth doing. Go over the stile and follow the river as it bends left. After 200 yards turn left away from the river across a broad plank bridge and diagonally left up the field to a hedge. Turn left for a few yards then over a stile onto a footpath. Turn right alongside the field, through a swing gate onto the lane and right, back to the pub. (1 mile)

Date walk completed:

WRENINGHAM, KETT'S COUNTRY AND THE TAS VALLEY WAY

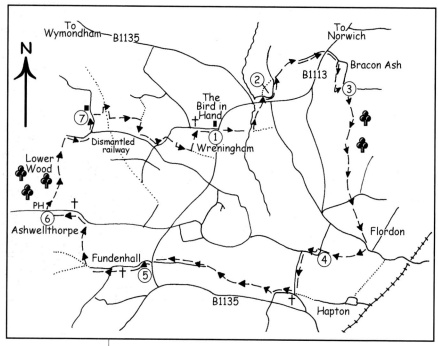

Distance:
10¾ miles

Map: OS Landranger 144 and 134 or Explorer 237

Starting Point:
The Bird in Hand pub.
GR 167988

How to get there: Wreningham is 7 miles south-west of Norwich. From the city take the A140 Ipswich Road then turn right on the B1113. After Bracon Ash, the Bird in Hand pub is on the right, on a corner of a minor road leading to the village.

ASHWELLTHORPE VILLAGE SIGN WITH ALL SAINTS' CHURCH BEYOND

*T*here are fast connections here – Lotus Cars has its headquarters at nearby Hethel, and Wreningham itself had a trotting track not too long ago. No rush when you get out there, however – indeed it would be a shame not to linger at the flint-built churches you pass, neat and unpretentious in churchyards scattered with wildflowers. The path also leads you across a lovely wooded common rich in wildlife and touches on two longer walks – Kett's Country named after Robert Kett, who led a peasants' rebellion in 1549 and was hanged at Norwich Castle, and the 18-mile Tas Valley Way, from the outskirts of Norwich to Attleborough.

The Bird In Hand pub has a sign that shows not the expected falcon but the wren from which the village is said to take its name. Its home is this mellow red-brick building which looks like a typical Norfolk farmhouse though it has, apparently, always been an inn. Built in the 1830s, it is Grade II-listed with a rustic yet elegant interior – plenty of beams, gleaming brass, wood or tiled floors and original brick fireplaces. After having the same family of landlords for 50 years, the inn was sold at auction in 1985 and delicensed to become a private house. The villagers, however, demanded their pub back and the present owners decided to reapply for a licence and opened it as a freehouse in 1989.

The stated aim is to provide pub food that is 'different', and a string of awards testifies to its success. A printed menu and a specials blackboard change daily to offer both traditional and exotic dishes, all home-cooked using fresh ingredients. Typical dishes include roasted pork fillet on a bed of sweet red cabbage; chargrilled, blackened halibut steak marinated in lime and cajun spices; sweet potato, leek and onion bake in cheese sauce.

Real ales *are Adnams Best, Woodforde's Wherry and Fuller's London Pride, with frequent guests. Outside there is a large, attractive beer garden. Telephone: 01508 489438.*

The Walk

① Turn left out of the pub car park, cross the B1113 and take a signed footpath ahead with a **Kett's Country** waymarker. At the bottom corner of the long field, turn right down steps, through a hedge gap and then along a path with a barbed-wire fence on the left. Cross a stream on a wooden bridge with a Norfolk County Council yellow marker, then turn diagonally left up a short slope. Now turn left on a broad track, keeping the hedge on your left. This opens out with cropfields rising to the skyline on your right. The track leads into a concrete underpass beneath the road and, after that, turn right with a Kett's arrow. After 20 yards turn left over a stile onto a lane and then right. (After heavy rain, this underpass can flood – enough to make it difficult to use. If so, climb the low fence to the right and go up the bank to the road. Cross and turn right on the grass verge then, after 200 yards, turn left at the crossroads onto **Cranes Road**.) (1 mile)

② Just before the lane runs into the main road, turn left on **Cranes Road**, passing **Hill Farm** on your left. After 300 yards, turn right through a gap in the hedge onto a footpath immediately before The Cottage. The path bends left behind the red-brick house along a field edge. Ten yards after a hedge begins on your right, turn right in front of a telegraph pole down a narrow, tunnel-like path between hedges. At the end, turn left and immediately right onto **Poorhouse Lane** (named at the other end) and at the junction with a main road, turn left into **Bracon Ash**. Cross the road and turn right just past the war memorial onto **Hawkes Lane**.

On the other side of the lane is the modern art sculpture of the 1994 Bracon Ash and Hethel village sign. There is no indication of any ash tree from where the name might have sprung, though the nearby Hethel Thorn is said to be 800 years old and claims to be the smallest nature reserve in Britain.

Where the lane bends sharply left, turn right on a path with one of the green **Upper Tas Valley Walk** markers that alternate with **Tas Valley Way** signs as far as **Flordon**. Keep ahead between hedges, following a yellow arrow into woodland. The path twists between trees and, after 20 yards, bends left. At the lane turn left and, after 150

THE BIRD IN HAND, WRENINGHAM

yards, right onto a dead-end lane. (1½ miles)

③ After 50 yards, where **Marsh Lane** bends left, keep ahead on a track to the right of a corrugated metal farm building. The track heads across open fields and, after going through a large hedge gap, turns diagonally left with a public footpath sign towards a hedge. Turn right along the field edge, go through a hedge gap between two tall trees and keep ahead. This path bends round a small pond, with woodland soon on your left. At the end of the field cross a plank bridge with a **Tas Valley** arrow and head across a cropfield. Pass through a hedge gap onto a grassy path then soon right and immediately left in front of a pretty red-brick cottage. At the lane turn right and, after 50 yards, left through the hedge with a footpath sign. At the bottom of the field turn right and left over a wooden bridge and stile. Keep to the left-hand edge of the field, over a stile, across a track with the farm on your left and ahead. Stay on the left of the field and at the bottom go over a stile onto a lane. Turn left into **Flordon** and, after 200 yards, turn right by a mapboard showing community paths, opposite the end wall of the former Olde Black Horse pub.

You now head across ancient Flordon Common, a wooded area interesting for its range of birdlife, butterflies and plants, including one stretch scented with wild mint and glowing with yellow flag irises in season.

The path crosses a broad plank bridge then twists and turns through trees, keeping close to the clear stream. At the end of the common, climb a stile with an interesting use of old metal cooking pots as fence-post tops and turn left onto a lane. (2 miles)

④ The lane turns sharply right and left (ignore **Marsh Lane** to the right) and climbs gradually. At the head of the slope, with Redwings horse sanctuary on either side, the tower of **Hapton church** comes into view. The lane bends right to pass **St Margaret's**, a simple flint church that, like so many in Norfolk, seems to grow out of the landscape. Where the lane bends sharply left, keep ahead on a broad track with a footpath sign and, shortly, an NCC marker. This soon passes above the bed of an old railway line, a favourite spot for green woodpeckers with their yaffling call. The track passes through open fields and is then hedged on the left. Where the hedge ends and the main track bends right, keep ahead on a grassy path with a small wood to the right. Soon cross the main road (**The Turnpike**) and head along **Church Lane** to **Fundenhall**. (1¾ miles)

⑤ Pass **St Nicholas' church** on the

left, whose rather stern exterior is softened in spring by primroses sprinkled over the grass. After 50 yards, where the lane bends left, keep ahead on an unsigned track passing a pink-washed cottage. After 200 yards turn right with a footpath sign and Kett's marker onto a grassy path heading across open fields to **Ashwellthorpe**. At the road, cross and turn left, soon passing **All Saints' church** and the unusual, totem-pole-like village sign made in 1977 to mark the Queen's Silver Jubilee. Just after a garage, turn right on a path signed 'Kett's Country' and 'NWT Nature Reserve'. (The White Horse pub is a few yards further along the road.) (1½ miles)

⑥ Turn right on a plank bridge immediately before **Lower Wood**, then soon left across a ditch with an NCC arrow. Follow the wood's edge round to the left and then go right at the field end. After 50 yards turn left on a wooden bridge over a ditch and right along the field edge. Turn right through a hedge gap and immediately left on a clear path. At the field's end, cross a ditch on a plank bridge and the path bends right and broadens with a wooden fence and whitewashed house on the left. When the path meets a lane, turn left. (1¼ miles)

⑦ After 300 yards turn right with a footpath sign and keep ahead with a plantation of young trees on the left (**Long's Wood**). The path bends left and then right down steps onto the old railway track and up steps on the other side. Turn right and left with a Kett's marker on a broad swathe of grass between young trees. This leads through a circular clearing with a bench and then bends to the left. At the next crossroads of paths, ignore the Kett's Country arrow pointing ahead and turn right. The grassy path soon bends right and left, passing a white house on the left. Follow a yellow arrow straight ahead across a meadow and turn right, keeping the hedge on your left and heading towards houses. Cross a plank bridge with a yellow arrow and keep ahead to the lane. Turn left and then, at a T-junction by the Wreningham village sign, left again on **Church Road**. After 200 yards, just past a large house, turn right on a signed path between trees. Cross a ditch then turn right and left along the field edge. After 200 yards turn left, with the hedge on your left and head straight for **All Saints' church**, with its attractive millennium clock. Turn right on the lane back to the pub. (1¾ miles)

Date walk completed:

TIVETSHALL ST MARY AND THE HUNDRED LANE

WALKERS STOP FOR A BREAK IN THE SHADE

Distance:
7½ miles

Starting Point:
The Old Ram pub
GR 178855

Map: OS Landranger 156 or Explorer 230

How to get there: *Tivetshall St Mary is 15 miles south of Norwich. Coming from that direction on the A140 Ipswich road, go past the turn for the village and the Old Ram pub sits on the right-hand side of the main road.*

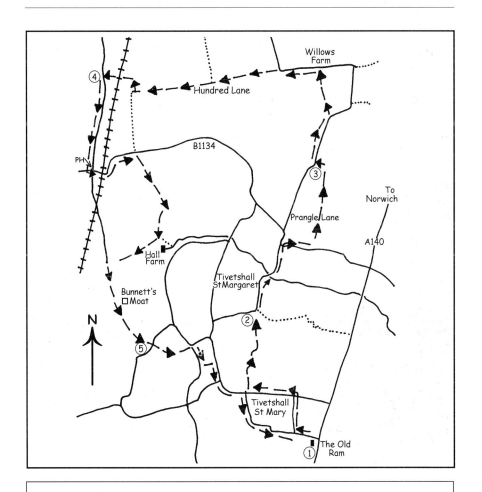

*B*etween two of Norfolk's main arteries, the London railway line and the busy A140 to Ipswich first laid by the Romans, lies an area of mixed arable farmland – cereals, peas, sugar beet, sweetcorn – crisscrossed by peaceful lanes, wildflower-fringed in summer. Starting close to the tiny twin villages of Tivetshall St Mary and St Margaret with their attractive old houses, this pleasant walk crosses the rail line (twice, in fact, for all you trainspotters) and passes by a maltings where the county's fine barley starts the process of becoming fine beer. Before that, it also takes in an unusually long stretch of ancient green pathway known as Hundred Lane.

87

The Old Ram is a lovely, Grade II listed pub that probably started out as a farmhouse in the 17th century but it has been a coaching inn for most of its life. Extensive stabling and a mention in *The Diary of a Country Parson* by James Woodforde testify to its popularity as a stopping point for travellers between London and Norwich.

The cream-washed exterior with its tall chimney stacks does not, somehow, prepare you for the atmosphere of elegant antiquity inside – a series of interconnecting rooms where all is mellow wood with a wealth of original beams and posts, exposed brickwork, red-tiled floors and Eastern carpets. Apart from the country-house-styled main room, there is a no-smoking dining room, a snug bar, a terrace room and a pleasant paved and flower-filled terrace with outdoor heaters.

Food on the regular and chef's specials menus is an interesting mixture of traditional and modern European, all prepared in-house using fresh ingredients. Fish is a speciality, with as many as eight seafood dishes on the daily menu, for example monkfish wrapped in Parma ham, sea bass fillet with red pepper and lime sauce, and plaice fillet topped with crayfish tails. The regular menu has a range of prime-cut Scottish steaks and there is a good vegetarian selection. An attractively priced over-60s daytime menu is available too. Food is served from 7.30 am to 9 pm with a range of breakfasts.

Real ales are Adnams Best, Woodforde's Wherry and Bass plus a guest, and 26 wines are served by the glass. Overnight accommodation is in 11 ensuite rooms.
Telephone: 01379 676794.

The Walk

a spring or winter walk with their broad wings flashing black and silver by turns.

The meaning of Tivetshall is reckoned to be 'lapwing nook' – presumably from the call that the birds make, as also found in their alternative name 'peewit'. As far as I know, 'tivet' does not survive as a Norfolk dialect word for lapwing, though the birds are still often to be seen in the county, brightening

① Turn right out of the large car park opposite the pub and head down **Ram Lane**. As I passed an animal enclosure on the left, a meek-looking Shetland pony there had a warning notice on the fence naming it as 'Buffy the Vampire Slayer' that bites people trying to stroke or feed it. A couple of donkeys in the next field were obviously not such vicious beasts. After 300 yards turn right on **Tinkers Lane** and, at the T-junction, left along the road past modern bungalows and then on a pleasant stretch where the verges are not overtidied and dog roses bloom in the hedgerows in early summer. Pass the **Tivetshall** sign at the start of **St Mary** and, after 100 yards, turn right through a hedge gap and on a plank bridge following a public footpath fingerpost. Head straight across the narrow meadow, cross a wooden bridge into the garden of Rose Barn and follow the yellow Norfolk County Council arrow on a path around the right-hand side of the grounds. The footpath originally ran straight through the garden, close to the house, and this is how it still appears on the Landranger map. In the summer of 2002 the path was diverted at the request of the householder, who explained to me in some detail that he was keen not to discourage walkers but thought it best if they did not wander all over his garden – or even picnic on his lawn – as had sometimes been the case in the past. At the end of the garden, cross a ditch on a plank bridge and then head across a field on a clear path to a yellow waymarker. Climb a stile, turning right and left along the field edge,

THE GRADE II LISTED OLD RAM INN

with the hedge on your right. At the field's end, turn right over a stile and plank bridge then left for a few yards to a lane. (1 mile)

②Turn right along the quiet lane, which immediately bends left and then after 400 yards turns sharp right and left past a house and a ford. If there is deep water here (it was dry as I passed), a wooden footbridge on the right can be used. Keep ahead on what is now **Star Lane** and at the next junction turn right onto the B1134. After a further 250 yards, turn left onto a grassy path following a public bridleway fingerpost. This appears on the Explorer map as **Prangle Lane** (Track), which is a generous description of its present, rather overgrown state. It is perfectly walkable though, and the rich variety of grasses and wildflowers attracts a range of wildlife.

As I paused for a drink on a hot, sunny day a painted lady settled briefly on my leg (the things that can happen to you on walks!) and other butterflies flaunting their beauty included red admirals and meadow browns.

The path leads first between cropfields, then alongside a hedge on the left as the going becomes easier and finally bends left and right to meet a lane. (1 mile)

③Turn right along the lane whose hedges are twined with wild honeysuckle in season. Where the lane bends right, just after **Lodge Farm**, turn left onto a footpath with a yellow arrow marker. Head diagonally left across the long field and then right along the field edge. At the end of the field, keep ahead on a path to meet a lane. If this last stretch is overgrown it might be easier to turn right at the end of the first field to the right-hand corner, then left into the next narrow field, skirting it anti-clockwise to emerge onto the lane.) Turn left on the lane, soon passing **Lost Lands** poultry farm on the right. After 150 yards, where the lane turns sharp right, keep ahead with a public bridleway fingerpost on a shady path, known as Hundred Lane, between hedges. Stay on this very pleasant path, which can be muddy at first but soon improves, for almost a mile, ignoring paths to left and right. As I passed, the scent of elderflowers was heavy on the air, and there was a good variety of birdlife and wildflowers to enjoy – also welcome opportunities for a rest stop on fallen tree trunks along the way. As you walk, you may well hear the sound of a train on the main Norwich-London line, and eventually the path bends right and shortly left to a gated crossing point over the rail tracks. (Before the railway line, a tempting-looking footpath on the map, off to the left, no longer exists.) Cross the train tracks and keep ahead on a broad unsurfaced lane. (2 miles)

④ After 100 yards, at a T-junction, turn left on the road, soon passing a large maltings on the left and at the next junction turn left onto the B1134, past the Railway pub and over the rail line again, this time on the road. Follow the road as it bends sharply left then right and after 250 yards, just before a power pylon, turn right with a fingerpost on a clear path which runs through a cropfield and then alongside a hedge on the left. At this point a partridge exploded from the densely packed stems of wheat just ahead of me in that heart-stopping way they have and whirred away. Soon the path bends sharply right away from the hedge to become a broader track, and gliders from nearby **Tibenham airfield** can be seen circling ahead. Just after passing a low corrugated-iron and wood building on the right, where the main track bends left, turn right on an unsigned track with hedges on both sides at first then only on the left. This leads to an unsurfaced lane with the thatched and pink-washed **Railway Farm** on the right. Turn left and the lane soon becomes a path along a field edge, passing under the power line (the last contact with these metal monsters).

To the left, opposite the pylon, is an ancient tree-screened feature known as **Bunnett's Moat**, which still holds water. The path soon bends left to meet a lane. (2 miles)

⑤ Turn left and, after 25 yards and opposite a large red-brick house, turn right on a plank bridge over a ditch and continue ahead with a ditch and woodland on your right. The path turns left, crosses the ditch and then heads left along a field edge with a hedge on the left. Just after passing a house on the left, where the path meets the bend of a lane, turn right on an unsigned footpath between hedges. Shortly after passing a path to the right, turn left on a path with a yellow arrow marker, through a cropfield to meet a lane. Turn right and follow the lane (**Rectory Road**) round to the left, signed 'Dickleburgh', then turn right onto **Bonds Road**. This bends sharply left (ignore Primrose Hill off to the right) and becomes **Ram Lane**, which leads back to the pub passing several lovely old cottages, including the splendidly named Frogs Pounce. I passed it warily, as I did Buffy the murderous Shetland pony just before the pub. (1½ miles)

Date walk completed:

SOUTHREPPS AND THE PASTON WAY

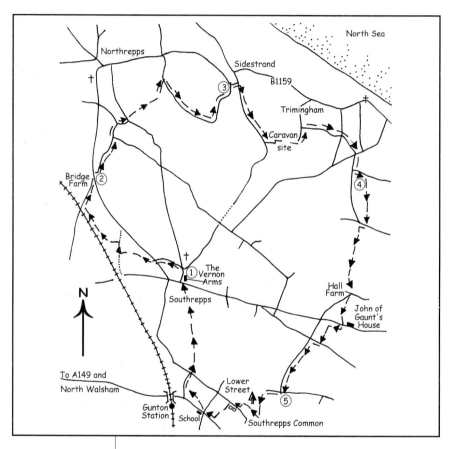

Distance:
9½ miles

Starting Point:
The Vernon Arms.
GR 257366

Map: OS Landranger 133 or Explorer 252

How to get there: *Southrepps is 4 miles south-east of Cromer, signed on a minor road to the east of the A149. From this direction the Vernon Arms pub is on your left on a junction in the village centre.*

THE VERNON ARMS WAS ONCE TWO FARM COTTAGES

*T*his area of North Norfolk just behind the coast, with its popular resorts of Sheringham and Cromer, has some of the most attractive landscapes in the whole county. The terrain is more varied than elsewhere, with rolling farmland and even (though, with my early walking done in the Peak District, I might have my tongue in cheek at this point) one or two hills. This walk reflects the variety on offer, with good grassy pathways, a couple of woodland stretches, a lovely little nature reserve and quiet lanes that are part of an experimental scheme designed to welcome people on foot, bike or horse.

The Vernon Arms has been formed from two traditional flint farm cottages thought to be upwards of 200 years old. However, its unassuming exterior is deceptive. Inside, the long main bar has games at one end and a strong farmhouse kitchen feel at the other, with tiled floors, two large brick fireplaces, exposed brickwork on the walls and stripped-wood tables. Off to one side is a most attractive non-smoking dining room and another small 'sun lounge'.

The name comes from Admiral Edward Vernon, who shot to fame in 1739 when he beat the Spanish in a major sea battle at Porto Bello in the Caribbean. Many pubs are named after him, which is perhaps not entirely apt since he was also credited with introducing the watered-down Navy rum ration that became known as grog, from his nickname Old Grog (apparently he wore a cloak made of a coarse cloth called grogram).

The pub's style in food is described as 'modern European' with good use of local produce including Cromer crabs and Gunton Park venison. The evening menu has such dishes as fillet of sea bass on a bed of garlic roasted vegetables, caramelised breast of Norfolk duckling served on sauerkraut, and baked tartlet of cherry tomatoes and red onion. The lunch menu is simpler, venison sausages on mustard mash being a favourite; there is also a good range of baguettes and omelettes.

> **Real ales** are Greene King IPA, Adnams Best Bitter plus one guest. No food is available on Sunday evenings in winter.
> Telephone: 01263 833355.

The Walk

NB: The owners of Woodland Leisure Park are happy for walkers to use the path through their caravan site though they would appreciate a phone call beforehand on 01263 579208 to let them know who is coming.

① Turn right out of the pub car park and up the street to the impressive, flint-built church.

The soaring mid-15th century tower of St James' church – at 117 feet the second tallest in North Norfolk – is a landmark for miles around. The base of the tower is richly decorated with the scallop shells of St James and the airy interior, with its lofty west window, a medieval 'angel window' and splendid beamed roof, is well worth a visit.

Turn left and soon, at the junction, keep ahead on **Clipped Hedge**

Lane, where the gardens of modern houses are generally in keeping with the name. After 300 yards cross **Sandy Lane** and take a track ahead with a public footpath fingerpost. Go over a stile by a metal gate, up steps with a yellow arrow and veer right on a clear path. This heads through a hedge gap and across another cropfield, at the end of which ignore the arrowed path ahead and turn right on a clear, unsigned path between hedges. After 200 yards turn left with a public bridleway fingerpost onto a grassy path that has fields stretching away to the skyline on your right. Drifts of cow parsley (or, if you prefer the more genteel yet still descriptive name, Queen Anne's lace) line the path in late spring, dotted with the bright flowers of red campion. The path bends right and broadens to run alongside the railway line (ignore a path to the right here) and meets a lane by a rail bridge. Turn right on the lane, soon passing **Bridge Farm** on your left. (1½ miles)

② Where another lane comes in from the right, turn right immediately after the junction onto a track, following a fingerpost. The track soon bends sharp left between grassy banks, with **Northrepps church tower** over to your left. After a dog-leg right and left, turn left at a T-junction, with a Paston Way marker among others.

THE SOARING TOWER OF ST JAMES' CHURCH, SOUTHREPPS

This waymarked path runs from North Walsham to Cromer and is named after the wealthy and enormously influential Paston family, who in turn took their name from the nearby village of Paston. An early story of rags to riches, the family rose from peasantry to aristocracy in two generations by taking advantage of the upheaval that followed the Black Death to acquire land. They are best known for the 15th century Paston Letters, the oldest surviving private correspondence between family members in Britain.

95

The track bends right past a handsome red-brick house to meet a lane. Now turn right, still on the **Paston Way**, and at the T-junction cross the lane onto a pleasant path that climbs gradually into woodland with violets in spring and early summer on grassy banks that make a good place for a rest stop. Soon the path opens out with views to the left before broadening and bending away from the wood. After 250 yards, as the main track of **Paston Way** continues round to the left, turn right on a grassy footpath with a yellow arrow. This is now a delightful path between hedged banks, rich in wildflowers, which soon runs alongside woodland at **Fox Hills**. The path turns sharp left away from the wood through open farmland with an expanse of sky all around and straight ahead a distant and tantalising view of the sea – this is as close to it as you get. (2 miles)

③ At the lane turn right and, after 50 yards, right again onto a 'Quiet Lane' signed to **Southrepps**. This is one of several such designated lanes in North Norfolk in a scheme to encourage walkers, cyclists and horse riders. Cars are still allowed, but if they do use these lanes they are expected to drive more slowly than normal and keep a sharp eye out for other road users. After about half a mile, just before the lane bends sharply right, turn left onto an unsigned track that soon passes a

house on the left and then twists left and right uphill into a caravan site. This is **Woodland Leisure Park**, attractively laid out among trees. At the end of the first field of the site, turn left onto a driveway between caravans and then, with the office and shops on your left near the entrance, turn right onto an unsigned track which meets a lane after about 600 yards. Cross and keep ahead on the track with a fingerpost and, at the junction, stay ahead on a lane signed 'Gimingham'. After 200 yards turn left on a lane signed 'Mundesley' and in 50 yards, by **The Grove**, right onto a marked path along the field edge. (1¾ miles)

④ The path climbs steadily with good views all round and then heads downhill to a narrow lane. Turn right and after 50 yards, just past an old flint barn, left with a fingerpost along a field edge. The path descends to a series of wooden bridges across a river and a dyke, then bends left across a field towards **Hall Farm**. Pass between gateposts, turn left on the track and right, up through the farmyard, to a lane. Turn right and immediately left onto a footpath marked '**Paston Way**' along a field edge with a hedge on the left. At the field's end, the path twists left and right to meet a lane, which you cross to enter the next cropfield. The path has now been diverted to turn right and left along the field edges. When it meets a lane, turn right and in 200 yards, after passing a farm and a house, turn left on a track with a bridleway fingerpost. (2 miles)

⑤ At a T-junction turn right onto a broader track, with a yellow arrow, which bends sharp left (ignore a narrow path ahead) past a modern flint house on the right and then on a footpath to the right of a track. Pass a large red-brick barn conversion on the left as the path heads towards woodland. Turn right and go over a stile by a metal gate into a sweet-smelling conifer wood then follow the yellow arrow to the right and head downhill, over another stile to emerge onto a broad track. Turn right, past a few old cottages, keeping an eye out for a noticeboard at the entrance to **Southrepps Common** on the left. Turn onto the boardwalk, which meanders through the attractive nature reserve with its reedbeds and show of wildflowers in season. Where the boardwalk forks,

take the left-hand path for a few yards to meet a lane. Turn right and at the crossroads keep straight ahead on the lane signed 'Gunton Station'. Opposite the far end of the school, veer right onto an unsigned footpath which is part-metalled at first then becomes narrower, heading through woodland. At the lane turn right, with the **Paston Way** arrow again, and at the T-junction cross and go over a stile onto a narrow path leading between houses at first then opening out to head along a field edge. The tower of **Southrepps church** looms large ahead now as the fields stretch away to the left (as I passed in late spring they looked, with their deep furrows, like an expanse of light-brown corduroy). Pass the bowls club and sports field on the left and into **Crown Loke** (Norfolk dialect for alleyway) with a Domesday plaque on the wall of a building to the left. The pub is now opposite you. (2¼ miles)

Date walk completed:

SHOTESHAM AND BOUDICA'S WAY

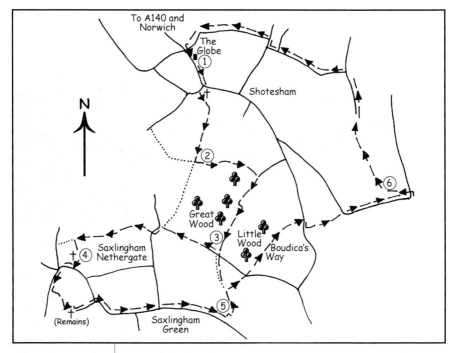

Distance:
9 miles

Starting Point:
The Globe pub.
GR 245994

Map: OS Landranger 134 or Explorer 237

How to get there: *From the Norwich southern bypass (A47) take the A140 Ipswich road and then either the first or second lane off to the left to pass through Stoke Holy Cross and then turn left to Shotesham. The Globe pub is on the left as you enter the village.*

THE IVY-COVERED RUIN OF ST MARTIN'S CHURCH, SHOTESHAM, WITH ST MARY'S JUST TO THE RIGHT

*B*attling Queen Boadicea of old has been reinvented, a suitable icon for our times perhaps, but despite the higher profile there is still a major uncertainty. Apart from the irritating matter of how to spell her new name – Boudica or Boudicca? – it's where exactly she had her base. Despite the sword markers that point your way as you cover stretches of the long-distance Boudica's Way from Norwich to Diss, there is no evidence she ever travelled this route. There is, however, a timeless feel to the lovely, rolling countryside, and as you stride out on broad paths alongside ancient woodland, it is not hard to picture the combative queen as she thunders past in her chariot. Just watch out for the knives on the wheels. . .

The Globe has such a peaceful setting, overlooking Shotesham Common, that it comes as a surprise to read in the village history that 'it wasn't unusual for one of the regulars, who had had a drop too much, to put his fist through the glass in the front door'. This was some 50 years ago, when, apparently, a barber would cut the locals' hair in the bar one night a week and 'it wasn't unusual to get some hair in your pint'. No wonder people felt like putting their fist through the door. . . Nowadays there are no such problems at the Globe, an attractive country pub dating back in parts to the 16th century, with a beamed, tile-floored bar, a 30-seat non-smoking restaurant and a friendly welcome for walkers.

The food here fits the place perfectly – home-cooked, traditional pub grub. The house speciality is Norfolk roll – layered sausagemeat, sage and onion, and apple – which is also served in a vegetarian version. Honey and herb chicken, and fish pie are among other main dishes, and a good choice of homemade puds includes Eton mess – meringue layered with fruit and ice-cream.

Real ales *are Greene King IPA and Adnams Best Bitter, both served direct from the cask, with an occasional guest. A large beer garden is behind the pub, and across the road a lovely seating area overlooks the common. The pub opens all day, but there is no food on Mondays.*
Telephone: 01508 550475.

 *The Walk*

① Turn left from the pub car park and along the lane, passing an assortment of attractive cottages, several of them thatched.

The water meadows of Shotesham Common on the right, rich in wild plants, give the village an unusual open and peaceful atmosphere. The village name derives from the Saxon Scots-ham – the settlement of 'Scots' or portions. These 12 divisions later amalgamated into four parishes and each, amazingly for such a small place, had its own church. All Saints' and St Mary's are still used, St Martin's is an ivy-covered ruin while nothing remains of St Botolph's.

After 300 yards turn right at the junction onto **Rogers Lane** and almost immediately left on a track between trees, with the tower of **All Saints' church** high above you. Apart from the fingerpost, there is here one of the yellow **Boudica's Way** sword markers you will see on much of the walk. The path leads into woodland, across a stream and uphill, soon with a barbed wire fence on the right. At the end of the wood, keep straight ahead on a clear path through a cropfield and then cross a plank bridge (perhaps a lack of respect here for our heroine as her marker is nailed to the floor for all to trample on). (1 mile)

There is now a good view across to St Mary's and, to the right of that, Hawes Green, where in 1771 the first cottage hospital in England was founded by former lord of the manor William Fellows. Its success led to a move to Norwich to form the first Norfolk and Norwich Hospital. You will see several wildlife conservation area signs – Shotesham Estates land is managed under a Countryside Stewardship Agreement and the unploughed field edges and broad paths are clear signs of this.

② At the field's end, turn left with the Boudica sword and the broad path skirts **Great Wood**, fine mixed woodland that appears on maps at least as far back as 1630 and was probably much larger. The path bends right and left with **Shotesham** nestling in its beck valley to the left. At the end of the wood turn right,

THE GLOBE, WHERE THE BARBER USED TO CALL

with a yellow public footpath arrow, on a lovely grassy path that climbs gradually. The path bends left and right, crossing a single plank bridge, before eventually turning left to leave the wood's edge. After 20 yards turn right onto an unsigned path through a cropfield, heading downhill to the right of an old red-roofed barn. (1 mile)

③ Turn right onto a narrow lane lined with snowdrifts of blackthorn blossom and yellow dog violets in spring and then, at a T-junction, left onto **Wood Lane**. This soon bends sharp right, and where it bends left again, keep ahead on a good path with a green Saxlingham Nethergate Circular Walks arrow, along the field edge. The land rises to the skyline on the left and the path eventually bends slightly right through a metal gate with a stile, across a damp meadow with a hedge on the left. After 200 yards turn left over a stile and left onto a path (ignoring signs to the right) leading up into the quiet churchyard of **St Mary the Virgin**. (1¼ miles)

This typically simple Norfolk flint church was begun in the late 11th century and is mentioned in the Domesday Book. Open during the daytime, it has a pretty interior with an elegant wooden screen and a porch with a bench that makes an excellent resting point. A sign on the green in front of the church has the date AD 832 for the village – Saxlingham Nethergate, along with nearby Saxlingham Thorpe and Green, has its origin as the home of Seaxel's people, and he took his name from the special battle axe, the 'seaxe', used by the Saxons.

④ Leave the churchyard through an iron gate and at the road turn right. Head into the village with its pretty colour-washed cottages and where the main road bends right, stay ahead until, after 50 yards, it becomes **Pitts Hill**. Now turn immediately left with a public bridleway fingerpost on a broad, sandy track that runs with water after heavy rain. After about 200 yards, at a crossroads of paths with a fingerpost, turn left with a Boudica sword (on the other side of the post) onto a grassy path that leads up a slope between banks. As the path levels, turn left at a multi-signed fingerpost, keeping trees on your right and a view over fields back to the village on the left. Soon this path runs into a broader track where you turn left and keep ahead to meet a road by Hill Cottage, a handsome cream-washed house with fine thatchwork. Turn right, again with the Boudica sword, onto the road and where this bends right just past Dairy Farm Cottage, turn left on a quiet lane signed 'Shotesham'. Stay on the lane (with walkable grass verge) as it crosses tranquil **Saxlingham Green** where the 'teecha teecha' call of great tits rang out as I passed, ignoring **Chequers Lane** to the left, past a large hall and a couple of other houses before turning left onto a path, still following Boudica. (1¼ miles)

⑤ Turn right and skirt a large field anticlockwise. Soon turn right with the sword, ignoring the path straight ahead, and go up the field, bending right to meet a lane. Cross this, onto a plank bridge and take the path straight across to **Little Wood**, with a pleasantly rolling wooded landscape away to the right. Turn right to skirt the wood, going over a stile and then a second stile onto a lane. Turn right and, after 50 yards turn left, with a fingerpost, on a path that climbs steadily through fields where skylarks sing, passing a small pond on the left and onto **Heath Road**. Turn right and follow the road as it bends left, signed to **Brooke**. The road bends sharp left then, as it takes a sharp right, turn left on a path with a fingerpost and Howe Circular Walks arrow. Head diagonally right across the field (the path is not very clearly defined) towards a wood. (2 miles)

⑥ Cross a plank bridge and turn right onto a delightful green lane which leads through a belt of woodland where it is a shame to hurry and eventually opens out on the left. Where it meets a lane, turn left past a large modern house and keep ahead to a junction. Keep ahead on the road signed Shotesham, then after 50 yards turn right at the T-junction and almost immediately left onto **Naidens Lane**. This was originally (and perhaps not surprisingly) called Maidens Lane, so named for the young girls who used to stroll along it, at the village end, after church. Why it changed, no one seems to know – one more Norfolk oddity. The lane soon becomes a track as it passes a farmhouse on the right. Ignore a footpath signed to the left and stay on this broad track, with good views on both sides as it bends left to skirt a wood. The path now bends right and you have earned the fact that the last stretch is downhill into the village. At the lane, turn left back to the pub. (2½ miles)

All Saints' church, which you passed at the beginning of the walk, has a commanding view over the common. On its belltower is a stone vulture, blessed among God's creatures with the keenest eyesight, which is said to be looking east for the Second Coming, but you don't have to go round again. . .

Date walk completed:

EAST RUSTON AND THE WEAVERS WAY

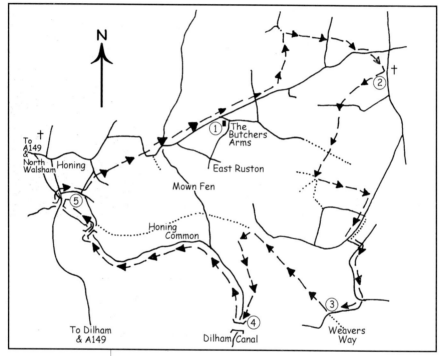

Distance:
8¼ miles

Starting Point:
The Butchers Arms pub.
GR 345283

Map: OS Landranger 133, 134 or Explorer 252

How to get there: East Ruston is 5 miles south-east of North Walsham. From the A149 follow minor roads signed to Honing (through Dilham if coming from Norwich), then to East Ruston. The Butchers Arms pub is on the right by a junction.

THE TONNAGE BRIDGE ACROSS DILHAM CANAL

To describe this as a quiet corner of Norfolk is to risk stating the obvious since there are so many of them in this still largely unspoilt county. There is, though, a genuine feeling of timelessness in the farmland and fenland of the East Ruston area with its stretches of rough grazing marsh and narrow, little-used lanes. The walk is one of contrasts – through cropfields at first, then on a fine stretch of the long-distance Weavers Way which is a haven for wildlife, before heading back alongside a peaceful and unusual waterway.

The Butchers Arms is a traditional whitewashed flint and tile pub, described by its landlady as 'quintessentially English'. It dates from the 16th century and was originally three flint cottages, the middle one run as a butcher's business. It was extensively renovated in 1988 without spoiling its character.

It sits in a lovely position overlooking a small green, with a shady patio and garden to one side and the old bowling green turned into a pleasant sitting/play area. Inside, there is a cosy feel to the long main bar with its beams and brasses and brick fireplace at each end. The small Acorn Restaurant is warmly decorated in deep pink with cane chairs and a larger restaurant is elegant in light blue.

Food at the Butchers is pretty well all homemade using local ingredients and fresh fish from Lowestoft. A lunchtime menu includes such dishes as steak, ale and mushroom pie; liver, bacon and tomato casserole; and vegetable lasagne. There is also a range of sandwiches (not Sunday), and from Monday to Friday a bargain dish of the day 'available to all, not just pensioners'. The pub, fittingly, does its own butchery, and the evening à la carte menu has a range of steaks including a 'Dragon rump of unknown weight'.

Real ales in this freehouse are Bass, Adnams Best, Butchers ale from Bass, plus a guest. The pub stresses that it has no TV, jukebox or pool table and takes only cash or cheques.
Telephone: 01692 650237.

The Walk

East Ruston takes its name from the Old English hris (brushwood) and means 'brushwood enclosure'. In White's 1845 Gazetteer of Norfolk it is described as a 'large, scattered village' and it seems so to this day, with no real centre and the surrounding fenland and alder carr giving it an undeveloped feel. As long ago as 1810, some 300 acres of land were allotted to the poor, who pastured their cattle on it and cut fuel. The allotment signs still stand opposite the pub.

① Turn right out of the pub car park onto the broader road (not sharp right onto **Oak Lane**). Pass the large area of **East Ruston Poors Allotment** on the left and stay ahead at the crossroads, passing the school and village hall. After a further 200 yards, turn left with a fingerpost onto a path along a field edge, where the hedge on the left soon gives way to open fields on both sides. At the end of the field, turn right at a marker post with yellow Norfolk County Council arrows along another field edge. As I passed, the spread of barley close to harvest shone a beautiful rich gold tinged with red. Ahead and to your left now, the tall tower of Happisburgh church and famous red and white striped lighthouse come into view. At the lane turn left and, after 50 yards, right onto a cropfield path, heading straight for another church – **St Mary's**. At the next lane turn left then, after 100 yards, right on an unsigned path across the corner of a field to the church. This short path was not clearly cut when I was here –

if it seems difficult, stay on the lane to the T-junction and turn right to the square-towered, castle-like church, no longer used for worship but maintained by the Churches Conservation Trust. (1¾ miles)

② Across the road from the church, follow a yellow arrow on a path that leads ahead along a field edge and soon bends left, with a marker, through a cropfield. Head straight across the next field, still with a yellow arrow, then cross a lane and keep straight ahead following a fingerpost and ignoring a yellow arrow pointing diagonally right. The path bends right between fields then

THE DELIGHTFUL BUTCHERS ARMS IN EAST RUSTON

crosses a track and leads ahead. A gentle slope, fancifully called **High Hill**, is now in front of you but before that, at a clear junction of paths in the middle of the cropfield, turn left. At the field's end, stay ahead with a yellow arrow, cross a track and then a narrow field, with a handsome thatched farmhouse to your left, towards a line of conifers. Go through the trees and over a low metal fence to the narrow lane, where you turn right, now following an East Ruston Circular Walks arrow. Where the lane bends sharply right, stay ahead on a grassy bridleway with a fingerpost. This soon meets a lane where you turn left and follow it round to the right, signed 'Stalham', as it leads through wooded **Brumstead Common**. The lane bends sharply left then left again as it leaves the trees, and after another 100 yards you turn right on a broad unsigned track with a hedge of tall trees on the left. After 50 yards veer right along the edge of a meadow with a reed-filled dyke on your right and soon you head up a slight slope to meet the **Weavers Way**. (2 miles)

③ Turn right onto the Way, which follows an old railway line here and is a splendid grassy track slightly raised above surrounding fields. Butterflies are abundant here in summer – whites, meadow browns, ringlets, speckled woods – and a pair of green woodpeckers looped away as I passed. The path leads through

grazing marshland and a shady wooded stretch before running behind a row of houses. Ignore a path to the right and, 50 yards after the houses end, turn left with a yellow arrow. Go over a plank bridge and ahead on a path that is not too clearly defined, across a meadow towards metal gates. After going through the pair of gates, turn sharp left alongside a hedged dyke with rough grazing meadow to your right. At the end of the field, go over a stile, now with a Broads Authority yellow arrow, and ahead through meadowland where tall grasses show a lovely range of colours in summer. At an old wooden fence head diagonally right, still with a Broads arrow, and go over a stile at the far side of the meadow on a path alongside the river – except that it isn't a river. (1½ miles)

You are now by the North Walsham and Dilham Canal, the only official canal in Norfolk, which was opened in 1826 as an extension of the River Ant and built wider than older waterways to allow the traditional sailing wherries to get to and from Yarmouth. It was 8¾ miles long from its junction with the Ant near Weyford Bridge to Antingham Ponds, north of North Walsham, and carried mainly manure, offal, flour, corn, coal and vegetables. It was not, however, a huge commercial success and struggled for many years before the wherry Ella made the last trip in 1934. It quickly silted up and now looks like a tranquil, slow-flowing river that has been here since time began.

④ Turn right to cross the canal on the brick-built **Tonnage Bridge**, where cargo was weighed and tolls paid, and turn almost immediately right with a fingerpost along the opposite bank. The delightful path now stays close to the waterway for a good distance, with alternate cropfields and wooded areas to the left, crossing plank bridges over ditches and through a miniature wooden gate to head across meadowland. Soon walk alongside an elaborate gated wooden bridge, which is redundant except when there is deep mud to the side. The path moves slightly away from the river through a meadow, then heads right on a plank bridge over a ditch and back towards the river. Go through another tiny wooden gate and veer left with a Dilham Circular Walks arrow on a path through trees by the river. This stretch is now like a tributary of the Amazon with its tangle of trees and undergrowth, and murky water that looks as though it must conceal alligators. None of those showed, but I did see the jewel flash of a kingfisher as it darted away

from me. The path leads to a wooden-railed bridge by the old brick-lined lock, where you cross the river then head over a second bridge to meet a lane. Turn left and immediately left to rejoin the **Weavers Way** on a woodland stretch, which eventually heads between the iron supports of a road bridge embossed with a clover leaf pattern. Turn immediately right off the main track alongside a wooden gate and head through trees to emerge onto a lane. (1½ miles)

⑤ A network of lanes crosses **Honing Common** here and you go more or less straight ahead to take the third lane counting from the left, which bends to meet the road signed to **East Ruston**. Follow this round to the left, still signed East Ruston, passing a No Through Road off to the right and at the next road junction turn right. After 30 yards turn left with a fingerpost on a path cut through a cropfield and at a marker post bear left with a yellow arrow. Cross the next field and, still with a yellow arrow, continue across one more field heading for a line of trees. Go down a few steps to a lane where you turn right, soon passing a lake on the right. Stay on the lane, ignoring a turn to the right, back to the pub. (1½ miles)

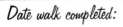

Date walk completed:

ROCKLAND ST MARY, THE RIVER YARE AND ROCKLAND BROAD

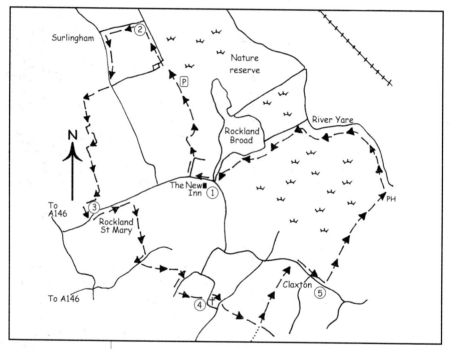

Distance:
9 miles

Map: OS Landranger 134 or Outdoor Leisure 40

Starting Point:
The New Inn
GR 328046

How to get there: *Rockland St Mary is 6 miles south-east of Norwich. From the Norwich southern bypass take the A146 Lowestoft road then the first left signed to Bramerton and from there follow signs to Rockland.*

ROCKLAND STAITHE

For walkers, the Norfolk Broads must remain largely a mystery. Few of these manmade lakes, dug out for peat in medieval times, have much access on foot and they are usually screened by dense vegetation. This walk, however, offers as its climax views over Rockland Broad that may not last long but give a real flavour of the rich boat and bird life they sustain. Before this, there is a long and interesting stretch beside the busy River Yare, a wonderful expanse of big-sky grazing marsh with its abundant wildlife, and excellent footpaths across rolling farmland that offer – unusually for Norfolk – fine views across the landscape.

The New Inn is a cream-washed early Victorian pub, in a lovely spot across the road from the staithe, and was indeed built as the new tavern. The old one, uphill in the main part of the village, was apparently deemed too far to go for the workers and boatmen connected with trade at the flourishing Rockland Brickworks. The boating interest was strong from the outset – one of the pub's early landlords, Jack Sayer, carried bricks to Yarmouth in his wherry *Louisa* and brought back Scandinavian timber. The mixture of new and old is still there in the contrast between the comfortable, traditionally-styled main bar with its wood panelling and the Mediterranean décor of the Signature restaurant in converted stables to one side.

The New Inn prides itself on cooking dishes from fresh ingredients, and there are two menus reflecting the different styles on offer. One has traditional pub grub such as fish and chips, a popular Cumberland sausage on mashed potato, plus an unusually wide range of baguettes and burgers. The other 'international cuisine' menu has such dishes as Greek lamb kleftico, confit of duck breast on beetroot mashed potato, and fusilli with roasted vegetables. There is an interesting approach to vegetarians – few dishes on the menu but they are encouraged to ask for favourites and the chef will do his best to deliver.

Real ales are Greene King IPA and Adnams Best Bitter, plus one guest. Food is served every day (all-day opening in summer), including breakfasts if booked in advance. There is a sheltered beer garden and overnight accommodation in two ensuite bedrooms.
Telephone: 01508 538395.

The Walk

① Turn left out of the pub car park and head up the lane. After 400 yards turn right on **Green Lane**, which soon turns into a broad track – bright with hawthorn blossom as I passed. A children's playground is on the right and beyond that you can see **Rockland Broad**. Go through a farmyard and keep ahead on a grassy path between fields; turn right at the field's end and left at the bottom of the slope alongside woodland. Pheasants scurry across the pleasant, grassy path here and the wood is rich in birdsong. The path broadens into a lane as it passes the **Ted Ellis Nature Reserve**, with grazing marsh stretching away on the right.

Ted Ellis was a writer, broadcaster, naturalist – keeper of natural history at the Castle Museum in

Norwich for 28 years – and great East Anglian character. For 40 years he lived here with his family at Wheatfen Broad in a remote cottage among 130 acres of woodland and fen. His widow Phyllis stayed on after his death and a trust was set up to preserve Wheatfen, one of the last tidal marshes in the Yare Valley and described by David Bellamy as being 'in its way as important as Mount Everest or the giant redwood forests of North America'. It is well worth a visit if you have time, though to do it justice will require an hour or so.

Stay ahead on the lane, passing **Grange Farm** on your left, then at the junction of roads turn left on **The Green** at **Surlingham**, signed 'Norwich'. (2 miles)

② Pass mainly modern houses with a few old cottages and at the next junction turn left on **Mill Road**, signed for **Rockland**. Head out of the village and take the next lane on the right. This is **Holloway Road** and after 400 yards you are free of the 'prison' of metalled road surface, turning left onto a grassy track with a footpath fingerpost. There are good views now over the wooded farmland stretching away to your

THE NEW INN, ROCKLAND ST MARY

right. The path dog-legs right and left round a copse then turns left and right along a field edge. I said good morning to the mawkins (scarecrows in Norfolk dialect) among the rows of peas but, as usual, forgot to prepare myself for the explosion of the bird scarer that startled me seconds later. The path bends right and left along another field edge then, just before houses, turns right and then left between houses to emerge onto the lane in **Upper Rockland**. (1¾ miles)

The village sign, just along the road to the right, gives the old title of Rokelunda, meaning 'rook grove' in Old Norse, a name shared with Rockland All Saints and Rockland St Peter 30 miles away to the west of Norwich, though there is no other connection between the settlements.

③ Turn left past the village shop and in 700 yards, just after a row of old cottages, a barn and a row of newer bungalows on the right, turn right onto a footpath between houses. There should be a fingerpost here though it had been broken off when I passed. The path between hedges soon opens out to head straight across a cropfield. At the field bottom, cross a plank bridge and stile over a ditch into a delightful damp meadow full of wildflowers and mint. Keep to the right-hand edge of the meadow on a path that is spongy in places. Cross a stream on a wooden bridge and head up a slope to meet a track. Turn right past a cottage and then immediately turn acutely left on a footpath with a fingerpost, up a slope between hedges where red campion and bluebells (some of them a pink variation) flourish in late spring. At a marker post with yellow arrows, keep ahead along a field edge, ignoring a path to the right. With rolling, wooded farmland away to the left, the path goes through a hedge gap and down a grassy meadow, bending right to meet a track. Turn left and, after 50 yards, at the T-junction of tracks turn right. This is a variation from the OS map, which shows a path heading straight up the field towards the church. After 100 yards turn left with a yellow arrow on a grassy path between fields and then with a hedge on the right. The path then heads through a hedge gap where you turn left and follow it round towards the church tower, emerging onto a lane by a striking flint-faced house that must, I guess, have been the vicarage. (1½ miles)

④ Go into the churchyard of **St Andrew's**, whose part-thatched roof seems slightly at odds with its solid, fortress-like tower. The path heads down the left-hand side of the churchyard but it is worth taking a minute for a look at the lovely, simple interior with its whitewashed walls and unusual wooden ceiling. At the bottom of the churchyard the path bends left and down a field edge to meet a sandy track. Turn right and almost immediately left before a low barn onto a track that heads gradually uphill, with fine views as it levels out. At the crossroads of paths, turn left with a bridleway fingerpost, keeping the hedge on your left. Away to your right now is the beet sugar factory at **Cantley** as the track broadens and heads downhill into **Claxton**. Turn right on the lane by a beautiful red-brick and thatched house and after half a mile, at the end of a green on the left called **The Warren**, turn left into **Mill Lane**. (1¼ miles).

⑤ The lane soon becomes a track, then you go over a stile onto a terrific grassy path that heads across the grazing marsh towards the river.

This is one of my favourite paths in the whole of Norfolk, with its wonderful sense of unchanging openness and great, gaping sky. It is, too, a birdlover's delight – no sooner had I climbed the stile on my last visit than I saw a kestrel hovering to my left and, ahead, a marsh harrier trying desperately to shake off a pair of mobbing crows. The scratchy song of sedge warblers is everywhere along the reed-fringed dykes, shelduck zoom

overhead and whitethroats dive into the hawthorn bushes.

When you reach the **River Yare**, turn left along the bank where there is immediately a welcoming stretch of grass for a rest stop. Also, if you detour to the right for a few yards here, you will find the **Beauchamp Arms**, another good pub with an excellent patio for boat-watching. Across the river, **Buckenham Marshes** stretch away to the railway line where the toy-like trains potter along to Yarmouth or Lowestoft. The path eventually bends left away from the river and runs alongside a channel to **Rockland Broad**. The 3mph signs here are for boats, not walkers – if you're still averaging more than that by now, you're doing well! The path bends left and right to skirt the broad and here are more birds to be seen, diving and skimming the water, including common terns and the much rarer black terns on passage. A bird hide on the right offers good views over the broad as you climb a stile with a Broads Authority arrow, then stay ahead on the raised path which bends left to meet the secluded inlet at **Rockland Staithe** with its moored boats. Cross the road back to the pub. (2½ miles)

Date walk completed:

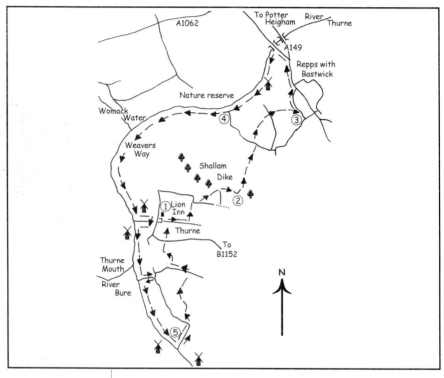

THURNE AND POTTER HEIGHAM

Distance:
8 miles

Starting Point:
The Lion Inn.
GR 404159

Map: OS Landranger 134 or Outdoor Leisure 40

How to get there: *Thurne is 16 miles east of Norwich. Take the A47 Yarmouth road, turn onto the A1064 at Acle, then left on the B1152. Thurne is signed left on a minor road and the Lion Inn is on the right in the village centre.*

THE LION INN, ONCE A VICTORIAN SHOOTING LODGE

*R*iverside walks in the Broads are among the best that Norfolk can give. There is a sense of unfettered space all around from the ancient grazing marshes dotted with the towers – and sometimes sails – of the old windpumps, and the river itself offers not only the interest of passing boat traffic but outstanding wildlife that is relatively easy to see. A wide range of birds and (in season) butterflies is on display as this walk first crosses open farmland and woodland, then gives a contrasting glimpse of the more bustling side of Broadland life before turning onto a long, yet invigorating stretch of the River Thurne.

The Lion Inn is an imposing double bay-windowed building near the river. It was originally a Victorian shooting lodge-cum-gentleman's residence and became a pub in 1935 when the licence was transferred from the nearby Red Lion. Inside the comfortable main bar and restaurant, there is a distinctly nautical feel with the wood-panelled walls, a ship's wheel over the fireplace and posts from the mast of a century-old sailing boat called the *Mayde* which belonged to a previous landlord.

Much used by holidaymakers and walkers, the pub aims to cater for a wide range of food tastes from traditional steaks to more unusual dishes. The house special, the Hungry Lion Feast, is certainly not one you'd want to tackle halfway through a walk – 8oz rump steak, 8oz pork chop, 8oz gammon, burger, jumbo sausage, grilled tomato, onion rings, mushrooms, peas and chips – but there are more delicate offerings on the blackboard, such as salmon paupiettes with smoked salmon mousseline. Other dishes include Mediterranean lamb, homemade steak and kidney pie and half a dozen veggie options. There are five different ploughman's and a good range of giant baps.

Real ales *are Woodforde's Wherry, Adnams Best and Fuller's London Pride with usually one guest.*
There is a sizeable beer garden and overnight accommodation in four bedrooms. Food is served all day, every day and the pub also runs a small shop.
Telephone: 01692 670796.

The Walk

① Turn left out of the pub car park and after 50 yards left onto a track with a **Weavers Way** fingerpost. Almost immediately enter a farmyard, turn left at the end of an old red-brick barn and the concrete track then bends round to the right, passing a house on your right. Keep straight ahead on the broad grass track between fields, ignoring paths to left and right, and after 300 yards turn left onto a footpath, unsigned but clear, along the field edge with a hedge on your left. Away to your left you now have the intriguing sight of boats on the **River Thurne** but apparently sailing across the fields. Soon keep straight ahead at the yellow arrow marker to meet a lane. Turn right here and, after 200 yards, left with a fingerpost on a path just before a modern house called Dingle Dell. Turn right behind the house and left along the field edge, with a yellow marker. At the end of the field keep ahead following a blue Broads Authority bridleway arrow, ignoring a path to the left. The pleasant, shaded path bends right, along the edge of woodland at **Shallam Dike** with a stream to the right. Wildflowers lined the path here on my summertime walk and the first of many peacock butterflies that day spread its wings to be admired. (1 mile)

② Follow the path as it bends left then crosses the dyke on a plank bridge. Cross a second wooden bridge, with a handrail and a yellow Broads Authority arrow, and veer left along the field edge. After 50 yards, at the end of the trees on your left, keep straight ahead on a path through a cropfield, heading for a fingerpost and smaller white marker post. Cross a narrow farm track and carry on ahead where there is a handwritten footpath sign on the white post, through a cropfield to a lane. Cross and keep straight ahead with a fingerpost on a broad grassy path between fields. Follow a yellow arrow to the right of a derelict brick and flint house and along a field edge with a hedge on your left. When the hedge ends, the path bends right across the field, across a track and ahead with a fingerpost on a clear path. Over to the right now is one of the round-towered churches that are such a speciality of Norfolk. The path bends right alongside a hedge and becomes a track leading to a lane. (1 mile)

THURNE DYKE MILL

③ With the attractive thatched cottage called Dere Holme facing you, turn left along the lane, passing modern bungalows on your right. At the junction with the main road at **Repps with Bastwick**, turn left on the pavement; this is a busy stretch, with holiday traffic hammering past all summer, but fortunately only a short one. At the sign for **Potter Heigham Bridge**, turn left off the main road onto the slip road and just before the bridge turn left to the riverbank.

The famous medieval bridge at Potter Heigham, with its rounded central arch and a pointed one at either side, still carries traffic over the River Thurne though the main road to Yarmouth has been rerouted. All around, boating businesses have sprung up and with them shops and eating places. There is a grassy area on the riverbank near the bridge which offers a handy rest and viewing point.

Turn left at the river along the path that leads through 'Chalet Land'. This stretch of holiday homes along the riverbank does seem to go on a bit, I grant you – No R84 is the last one if you're wondering – but it does offer some interest if, like me, you're amused by the names people choose to give their proudest possessions. Kingfishers and Terns I can understand, Merridays smacks somewhat of Enid Blyton though is hopefully true for the owners, but St Merryn and San Marino? Why? Would the owners rather be there than here? If so. . .

If the (very well kept, it has to be said) chalets are absolutely not to your taste, just cast your gaze to the left across the expanse of grazing marshland that has remained pretty well unchanged for centuries. There is an attractive black tower of an old windmill on the left; then, where a lane comes in from the left, there is another riverbank picnic spot and not far beyond that the holiday homes do eventually come to an end. (1¾ miles)

The stretch of countryside ahead is rich in birdlife. The yelping calls of coots on the river will keep you company as you walk, and you will almost certainly see, too, great crested grebes with their stunningly beautiful orange-gold head feathers and black tufts. It was because of this rich plumage that the RSPB was founded, by a group of Victorian ladies distressed at the slaughter of birds to supply the fashion for hat decoration. From the reed-edged dyke below to your left you will doubtless hear in spring and summer the strange song of sedge warblers, part melodious, part scratchy and spluttery. It is much harder actually to see one of the singers, though if you catch a glimpse of one perched on a bush or swaying on a reed, the broad, pale stripe above the eye will identify it.

④ Now a lovely stretch of the reed-fringed **River Thurne** lies ahead. The great feeling of openness is ample compensation for a footpath that can be decidedly lumpy going in places. At the white tower of **Thurne Dyke Mill** (more accurately a windpump, built in 1820 to lift water off the marshes in its scoopwheel and into the river), you have to turn left along the staithe to **Thurne** village. You are now very close to the starting point and could finish the walk here, or just have a rest and a drink at the Lion, but if you don't like touching base during a walk, turn right up the other side of the inlet, over a stile and onto the riverbank again. The path is now easier for a while before the **Thurne** meets the broader **River Bure**, coming in from the right. Another inlet you now have to skirt offers a further opportunity for a connoisseur of names, this time boats. *Ragtrade*, I guess, was where the owner made his money, *Tallullah* suggested visions of a showbiz lifestyle but my favourite, as a summing-up of the pleasures of escapism, was *The Alternative*. (2½ miles)

⑤ Just after a windmill to your right across the river, turn left alongside another inlet. At the end, go through a gate, ignore a path to the left but turn right and immediately left along the far side of a narrow dyke. After a few yards bend away from the dyke with a Weavers Way arrow, pass to the side of a metal gate and ahead on a concrete track. After 100 yards turn left, still following a Weavers Way marker (the 'No Access' notice applies only to cars), enter a farmyard and keep to the right of the house and barns. At the Weavers Way arrow, turn right away from the fence and head across the meadow towards a marker post. The path bends right, now also with a Broads Authority arrow, between open fields under a vast skyscape. Turn left along a concrete track with a fingerpost, after 200 yards right along the field edge and a further 100 yards left, still with a Weavers Way arrow, then right again to the church. At the lane, turn left and immediately right on a grassy path alongside the church and then a field edge. Climb two stiles fairly close together, then turn left on the track, retracing your steps from earlier in the day through the farmyard and right to the pub. (1¾ miles)

Date walk completed:

HALVERGATE MARSHES
AND BREYDON WATER

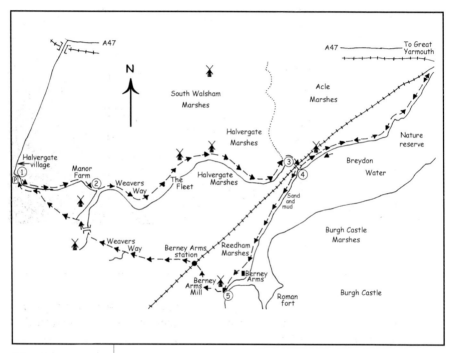

Distance:
11¼ miles or
7¼ miles

Starting Point:
The lane near
Halvergate.
GR 428068

Map: OS Landranger 134 or Outdoor Leisure 40

How to get there: *The walk starts about 6 miles west
of Great Yarmouth, near Halvergate village. Take the A47
and about 2½ miles east of the roundabout at Acle, turn
off southwards on a minor road signed to Halvergate. At
a T-junction after a long, straight stretch, turn left and
almost immediately park on the grass verge on the right.*

BERNEY ARMS MILL BY THE RIVER YARE

*T*he expanse of traditional grazing marsh between Halvergate and Yarmouth, veined by countless narrow dykes, is the nearest Norfolk comes to wilderness. This is certainly not the place to be caught by a winter storm, and even during the rest of the year there is an element of adventure. Virtually no shade against sun, or shelter against rain, make suitable clothing doubly important. Yet this walk has so much to offer – the beauty of the lonely marsh with its abundance of wildlife, a riverside path in a world of boats and windmills, but above all a wonderful sense of freedom that makes you feel glad to be alive. This route, most of it on the Weavers Way, starts near Halvergate village and takes you to the Berney Arms at the south-west end of Breydon Water for a lunchtime break (March to October).

The Berney Arms has surely the most unusual setting in Norfolk – perhaps in the country. Reachable on foot, by rail (to within a few hundred yards) and boat along the Yare, it has no access by road. Busy during the summer months with walkers and boating folk, it is closed from the beginning of November to the end of February when the bitter east winds can make Halvergate Marshes an inhospitable place indeed.

The building was originally a farmhouse and is now a practical, no-nonsense sort of pub. Its compact main bar, appropriately, has the atmosphere of a ship's cabin – dark wood-panelled walls, boat-like settles, ship's lamps and display cases of knots and nautical brasses. There are two games rooms and at the back a non-smoking dining room leads out to an attractive, decked patio overlooking a small garden. There are also tables on the riverbank giving good views of the boat traffic.

Food is substantial and traditional pub grub, with suet puddings of beef and horseradish, lamb and mint, steak and kidney a speciality. There are daily roasts of lamb, beef, pork or chicken, a range of grilled meats, and cod or plaice in beer batter. Veggie options include leek and mushroom crumble and chilli bean casserole, and a good range of sandwiches and baguettes is also on offer.

Real ales *include regulars Woodforde's Wherry and Greene King IPA plus a guest such as Brakspear.*
If you want to use the pub towards the beginning or end of its season, it would be advisable to check on opening times as these can be irregular.
Telephone: 01493 700303.

The Walk

① Keep straight ahead on the lane in the direction your car is pointing, past a farm on the left with an interesting assortment of redundant machinery outside. Stay ahead as it becomes a broad track with a public bridleway fingerpost, ignoring a **Weavers Way** arrow pointing right – this is the return path. You now have grazing marshland all around you, with the distant stream of traffic on the A47 away to the left the only point of contact with the modern world, it seems. As many as a dozen windmills (most of them, more accurately, windpumps) are in view and birds are everywhere – a charm of goldfinches feeding on thistle heads, the mournful call of a curlew and, quite possibly, a marsh harrier drifting low in the distance. Pass **Manor Farm**, almost hidden in its clump of trees, and the path then bends sharply right with one of the **Weavers Way** markers that will guide you virtually all the way from here. (1 mile)

The Weavers Way is a 56-mile route, looping inland between Cromer and Yarmouth, whose name harks back to the days when the woollen trade made a large area of Norfolk extremely rich and produced its abundance of substantial churches in small villages.

② The track bends left, becoming narrower and grassier, often with scores of dragonflies and damselflies zooming about. Go through a metal gate and keep ahead, ignoring a path veering off to the right, and the track soon bends sharply left and right through another metal gateway, still with the **Weavers Way** arrow. The path bends right, with a sail-less windpump not far off to the left (a cormorant was sunbathing on top of this as we passed) and heads for a second one, to which you come much closer. The **Fleet waterway** is now just to your right as the lovely grassy path passes a house to the left and shortly one to the right (who could live in a house like these?). Go over a stile by a metal gate and keep

THE BERNEY ARMS, ACCESSIBLE ONLY BY TRAIN, BOAT AND ON FOOT

straight ahead across a track, as the path then crosses the water to meet a concrete track. (2½ miles)

③ Turn right onto the track with a **Weavers Way** fingerpost all but hidden in a bush and veer left and right to meet the single-track railway line from Norwich to Yarmouth. Go through the gates to cross the line, then turn left over a stile and up the bank where the silver expanse of **Breydon Water** is now suddenly and dramatically spread out before you. (If you wish to take the shorter option, turn right after crossing the railway line and over a stile onto the bank, then ahead.) To do the full distance of the walk you now stay on the bank, with Yarmouth stretched along the skyline over the water, until you reach the railway line again after almost two miles. Here you turn round and retrace your steps, staying ahead on the bank with the tall, black tower of **Berney Arms Mill** ahead. Covering the same ground like this is not something I normally want to do, but this is such an outstanding walk alongside **Breydon Water** – especially recommended for the birdwatchers and boat-lovers among you – that it is well worth tackling, and there is no way of making it a circular route. The concrete-reinforced bank has a good covering of grass that makes it easy walking and you can, of course, do as much or as little of this section as you wish, depending on the time, the weather etc, before turning back. (4 miles).

As you enter the stretch of bank leading to the pub, the Berney Marshes RSPB reserve is now laid out before you – a fairly recent scheme by the Society, which was concerned about the strong possibility of the grazing marshes being turned into arable land to the detriment of the bird population. Land has been bought, and its management includes water being pumped onto some fields in winter, to be held by low dams. The result is an impressive total of birds, among them small numbers of breeding ruff and black-tailed godwits and thousands of ducks, geese and swans in winter. Behind the Berney Arms there is a screen and birdwatching seat looking out over Seago's Marsh, named after Michael Seago, a noted local naturalist and writer.

④ **Breydon Water** is busy with pleasure boats heading up and down the main channel as you pass. Birds, too, make good use of it, especially at low tide when the exposed mudflats attract hundreds of waders and regularly such unusual species as spoonbill and little egret. Across the water you can see the ruins of **Burgh Castle** – the Roman fort of Gariannonum built in about AD 280 as part of the so-called Forts of the Saxon Shore to protect south-east

England from seaborne raiders. You reach the **Berney Arms** just at the point where the rivers Yare and Waveney meet and have doubtless earned a rest by this stage (but, remember, the pub is closed in the winter months). Go past the next-door general shop and after about 200 yards you come to the imposing mill. (1½ miles)

Berney Arms Mill was built in the middle of the 19th century – not to pump water this time but to grind clinker for a nearby cement works, though it did later serve as a pumping station. At around 65 feet, it is the tallest marsh mill in Norfolk and is still in working order. There are picnic tables in a grassy area here and the mill itself is open from 1 April to 30 September.

(5) Pass the mill and turn immediately right over a stile onto a track, leaving this to veer left following the rather incongruous 'railway station' arrows. Go through a wooden gate and on a path over the meadow that is not too clearly defined but veers slightly left, heading for the station board which sticks up against the sky. Go through a wooden gate and across the railway line with the platform of **Berney Arms halt** to the right – this is, amazingly, a request stop! Keep ahead with a **Weavers Way** marker

and a dyke on your left, heading for a wooden gate. Turn left through the gate across the dyke and immediately right through another gate, now keeping close to the dyke on your right. Soon ignore the first crossing point, then turn right over the dyke and head diagonally left over the meadow, straight towards a distant windmill. Go through a wooden gate with a **Weavers Way** marker and ahead on a plank bridge with a handrail. Turn left and after 20 yards right over a stile, then diagonally left over the meadow, heading straight for gates with a red-roofed building in a clump of trees behind. Go through double metal gates and ahead, ignoring a path veering right, still heading for the clump of trees. Go over a stile and veer right towards the mill again, soon turning left over a stile and on a wooden bridge across the river. Turn right and the path then bends left alongside a dyke for a few yards before you turn right on a concrete bridge (the stile here doesn't properly connect and you have to go between railings onto the bridge). Turn left, now with the weed-covered dyke on your left, and after a lovely stretch the path bends right through a tiny wooden gate alongside a metal gate, over a stile and you turn left on the lane back to your car. (2¼ miles)

Date walk completed: